First Workshop on Multilingual Surface Realisation (SR'18)

Shared Task and Beyond

Held at ACL 2018

Melbourne, Australia
19 July 2018

ISBN: 978-1-5108-6723-9

ACL 2018

Multilingual Surface Realisation: Shared Task and Beyond

Proceedings of the Workshop

July 19, 2018
Melbourne, Australia

Introduction

Natural Language Generation (NLG) is in the ascendant both as a stand-alone (data-to-text or text-to-text) task and as part of downstream applications such as abstractive summarization, dialogue-based interaction, question answering, etc. Only in 2017, three "deep" NLG shared tasks that focused on language generation from abstract semantic representations have been organized, although for English only. Surface realization is also a burning issue, in particular, in view of the recent creation of multilingual treebanks annotated with Universal Dependencies (UD). The Multilingual Surface Realization Shared Task (SR '18), whose outcome is presented in these proceedings, targets surface realization from data released for the recent CoNLL shared task on multilingual parsing to UDs. After the First Surface Realization Shared Task in 2011, which focused on English, SR '18 is the second shared task on surface realization and the first to target multilingual input. 21 teams registered for SR '18, and eight of them submitted outputs of their systems.

These proceedings include an overview of SR '18 and the description of the eight participating systems, which will be presented at the workshop. We are pleased that for the workshop we could also win Hadar Shemtov, Head of NLG, dialog and summarization groups at Google Research, as invited speaker. We trust that overall the workshop will be a forum for fruitful discussion, and that it will give an impetus to further advances and to further shared tasks in the field.

The workshop organizers

June 2018

Organizers:

Anja Belz, University of Brighton, UK
Bernd Bohnet, Google Research, UK
Yvette Graham, Dublin City University, Ireland
Simon Mille, Pompeu Fabra University, Spain
Emily Pitler, Google Research, USA
Leo Wanner, Pompeu Fabra University, Spain

Program Committee:

Miguel Ballesteros, IBM Research, USA
Anders Björkelund, University of Stuttgart, Germany
Johan Bos, University of Groningen, Netherlands
Robert Dale, Macquarie University, Australia
Katja Filippova, Google Research, Switzerland
Claire Gardent, CNRS, LORIA, France
Kim Gerdes, Sorbonne Nouvelle, France
Yannis Konstas, Heriot Watt University, UK
Emiel Krahmer, Tilburg University, Netherlands
Mirella Lapata, University of Edinburgh, UK
Jonathan May, Information Sciences Institute, USA
David McDonald, Sift Inc., USA
Ryan McDonald, Google Research, USA
Detmar Meurers, University of Tübingen, Germany
Alexis Nasr, University of Aix Marseille, France
Joakim Nivre, Uppsala University, Sweden
Stephan Oepen, University of Oslo, Norway
Horacio Saggion, Pompeu Fabra University, Spain
Lucia Specia, University of Sheffield, UK
Kees Van Deemter, University of Aberdeen, UK
Sina Zarrieß, University of Bielefeld, Germany
Yue Zhang, Singapore University of Technology and Design, Singapore

Invited Speaker:

Hadar Shemtov, Google Research, USA

Table of Contents

Workshop Program

8:45–9:00   **Opening**

9:00–10:00   **Invited Talk**
Hadar Shemtov

10:00–10:30   *The First Multilingual Surface Realisation Shared Task: Overview and Evaluation Results*
Simon Mille, Anja Belz, Bernd Bohnet, Yvette Graham, Emily Pitler, Leo Wanner

10:30–11:00   **Coffee break**

11:00–12:30   **Oral session 1**
11:00–11:30   *BinLin: A Simple Method of Dependency Tree Linearization*
Yevgeniy Puzikov and Iryna Gurevych

11:30–12:00   *IIT (BHU) Varanasi at MSR-SRST 2018: A Language Model Based Approach for Natural Language Generation*
Shreyansh Singh, Ayush Sharma, Avi Chawla and A.K. Singh

12:00–12:30   *Surface Realization Shared Task 2018 (SR18): The Tilburg University Approach*
Thiago Castro Ferreira, Sander Wubben and Emiel Krahmer

12:30–13:45   **Lunch break**

13:45–14:15   **Oral session 2**
13:45–14:15   *The OSU Realizer for SRST '18: Neural Sequence-to-Sequence Inflection and Incremental Locality-Based Linearization*
David King and Michael White

14:15–15:30   **Poster session**
Generating High-Quality Surface Realizations Using Data Augmentation and Factored Sequence Models
Henry Elder and Chris Hokamp
AX Semantics' Submission to the Surface Realization Shared Task 2018
Andreas Madsack, Johanna Heininger, Nyamsuren Davaasambuu, Vitaliia Voronik, Michael Käufl and Robert Weißgraeber

NILC-SWORNEMO at the Surface Realization Shared Task: Exploring Syntax-Based Word Ordering using Neural Models
Marco Antonio Sobrevilla Cabezudo and Thiago Pardo

The DipInfo-UniTo system for SRST 2018
Valerio Basile and Alessandro Mazzei

15:30–16:00   **Coffee break**

16:00–17:30   **Panel, Discussions**

The First Multilingual Surface Realisation Shared Task (SR'18): Overview and Evaluation Results

Simon Mille
UPF, Barcelona
simon.mille@upf.edu

Anja Belz
University of Brighton
a.s.belz@brighton.ac.uk

Bernd Bohnet
Google Inc.
bohnetbd@google.com

Yvette Graham
ADAPT Research Centre, DCU
graham.yvette@gmail.com

Emily Pitler
Google Inc.
epitler@google.com

Leo Wanner
ICREA and UPF, Barcelona
leo.wanner@upf.edu

Abstract

We report results from the SR'18 Shared Task, a new multilingual surface realisation task organised as part of the ACL'18 Workshop on Multilingual Surface Realisation. As in its English-only predecessor task SR'11, the shared task comprised two tracks with different levels of complexity: (a) a shallow track where the inputs were full UD structures with word order information removed and tokens lemmatised; and (b) a deep track where additionally, functional words and morphological information were removed. The shallow track was offered in ten, and the deep track in three languages. Systems were evaluated (a) automatically, using a range of intrinsic metrics, and (b) by human judges in terms of readability and meaning similarity. This report presents the evaluation results, along with descriptions of the SR'18 tracks, data and evaluation methods. For full descriptions of the participating systems, please see the separate system reports elsewhere in this volume.

1 Introduction and Task Overview

Natural Language Generation (NLG) is attracting growing interest both in the form of end-to-end tasks (e.g. data-to-text and text-to-text generation), and as embedded component tasks (e.g. in abstractive summarisation, dialogue-based interaction and question answering).

NLG research has been given a boost by two recent developments: the rapid spread of neural language generation techniques, and the growing availability of multilingual treebanks annotated with Universal Dependencies[1] (UD), to the point

where as many as 70 treebanks covering about 50 languages can now be downloaded freely.[2] UD treebanks facilitate the development of applications that work potentially across all languages for which UD treebanks are available in a uniform fashion, which is a big advantage for system developers. As has already been seen in parsing, UD treebanks are also a good basis for multilingual shared tasks: a method that works for some languages may also work for others.

The SR'18 task is to generate sentences from structures at the level of abstraction of outputs in state-of-the-art parsing, encouraging participants to explore the extent to which neural network parsing algorithms can be reversed for generation. SR'18 also addresses questions about just how suitable and useful the notion of universal dependencies—which is in the process of becoming the dominant linguistic formalism across a wide range of NLP applications, parsing in particular—is for NLG. SR'18 follows the SR'11 pilot surface realisation task for English (Belz et al., 2011) which was part of Generation Challenges 2011 (GenChal'11), the fifth round of shared-task evaluation competitions (STECs) involving the language generation tasks.

Outside of the SR tasks, just three 'deep' NLG shared tasks focusing on language generation from abstract semantic representations have been organised to date: WebNLG[3] (Gardent et al., 2017), SemEval Task 9[4] (May and Priyadarshi, 2017), and E2E[5] (Novikova et al., 2017). What is more, these

---

[1] http://universaldependencies.org/

[2] See the recent parsing shared task based on UDs (Nivre and de Marneffe et al., 2016): http://universaldependencies.org/conll17/.

[3] http://talc1.loria.fr/webnlg/stories/challenge.html

[4] http://alt.qcri.org/semeval2017/task9/

[5] http://www.macs.hw.ac.uk/InteractionLab/E2E/

Proceedings of the First Workshop on Multilingual Surface Realisation, pages 1–12
Melbourne, Australia, July 19, 2018. ©2018 Association for Computational Linguistics

tasks have only been offered for English.

As in SR'11, the Multilingual Surface Realisation shared task (SR'18) comprises two tracks with different levels of difficulty:

Shallow Track: This track starts from genuine UD structures in which word order information has been removed and tokens have been lemmatised. In other words, it starts from unordered dependency trees with lemmatised nodes that hold PoS tags and morphological information as found in the original treebank annotations. The task amounts to determining the word order and inflecting words.

Deep Track: This track starts from UD structures from which functional words (in particular, auxiliaries, functional prepositions and conjunctions) and surface-oriented morphological and syntactic information have been removed. In addition to what is required for the Shallow Track, the task in the Deep Track thus also requires reintroduction of the removed functional words and morphological features.

In the remainder of this paper, we describe the data we used in the two tracks (Section 2), and the evaluation methods we used to evaluate submitted systems (Sections 3.1 and 3.2). We then briefly introduce the participating systems (Section 4), report and discuss evaluation results (Section 5), and conclude with some discussion and a look to the future (Section 6).

2   Data

To create the SR'18 training and testing data, we used as data sources ten UD treebanks for which annotations of reasonable quality were available, providing PoS tags and morphologically relevant markup (number, tense, verbal finiteness, etc.): UD_Arabic, UD_Czech, UD_Dutch, UD_English, UD_Finnish, UD_French, UD_Italian, UD_Portuguese, UD_Russian-SynTagRus and UD_Spanish-AnCora.[6] We created training and test data for all ten languages for the Shallow Track, and for three of the languages, namely English, French and Spanish, for the Deep Track.

Inputs in both Shallow and Deep Tracks are trees, and are released in CoNLL-U format, with no meta-information.[7] Figures 1, 2 and 3 show

a sample original UD annotation for English, and the corresponding shallow and deep input structures derived from it.

To create inputs to the Shallow Track, the UD structures were processed as follows:

1. Word order information was removed by randomised scrambling;

2. Words were replaced by their lemmas.

For the Deep Track, the following steps were additionally carried out:

3. Edge labels were generalised into predicate/argument labels, in the PropBank/NomBank (Palmer et al., 2005; Meyers et al., 2004) fashion. That is, the syntactic relations were mapped to core (A1, A2, etc.) and non-core (AM) labels, applying the following rules: (i) the first argument is always labeled A1 (i.e. there is no external argument *A0*); (ii) in order to maintain the tree structure and account for some cases of shared arguments, there can be inverted argument relations; (iii) all modifier edges are assigned the same generic label *AM*; (iv) there is a coordinating relation; see the inventory of relations in Table 1.

4. Functional prepositions and conjunctions in argument position (i.e. prepositions and conjunctions that can be inferred from other lexical units or from the syntactic structure) are removed (e.g. *by* and *of* in Figure 2); prepositions and conjunctions retained in the deep representation can be found under a *A2INV* dependency; a dependency path *Gov AM →Dep A2INV → Prep* is equivalent to a predicate (the conjunction/preposition) with 2 arguments: *Gov ← A1 Prep A2 → Dep*.

5. Definite and indefinite determiners, auxiliaries and modals are converted into attribute/value pairs, as are definiteness features, and the universal aspect and mood features[8], see examples in Figure 3.

6. Subject and object relative pronouns directly linked to the main relative verb are removed (and instead, the verb is linked to the antecedent of the pronoun); a dummy pronoun

---

[6]universaldependencies.org

[7]http://universaldependencies.org/

format.html

[8]http://universaldependencies.org/u/feat/index.html

```
1   The       the         DET     DT    Definite=Def|PronType=Art                              2     det          _   _
2   third     third       ADJ     JJ    Degree=Pos|NumType=Ord    5        nsubj_pass           _   _
3   was       be          AUX     VBD   Mood=Ind|Number=Sing|Person=3|Tense=Past|VerbForm=Fin   5     aux          _   _
4   being     be          AUX     VBG   VerbForm=Ger       5        aux_pass                     _   _
5   run       run         VERB    VBN   Tense=Past|VerbForm=Part|Voice=Pass         0    root    _   _
6   by        by          ADP     IN    _        8        case       _   _
7   the       the         DET     DT    Definite=Def|PronType=Art          8        det          _   _
8   head      head        NOUN    NN    Number=Sing        5        obl        _   _
9   of        of          ADP     IN    _        12       case       _   _
10  an        a           DET     DT    Definite=Ind|PronType=Art          12       det          _   _
11  investment            investment    NOUN    NN         Number=Sing        12       compound         _   _
12  firm      firm        NOUN    NN    Number=Sing        8        nmod       _        SpaceAfter=No
13  .         .           PUNCT   .     _        5        punct      _   _
```

Figure 1: A sample UD structure in English.

```
1   the         _    DET     DT    Definite=Def|PronType=Art                  _    2     det      _   _
2   third       _    ADJ     JJ    Degree=Pos          _        3    nsubj_pass           _   _
3   run         _    VERB    VBN   Tense=Past|VerbForm=Part          _        0    ROOT     _   _
4   be          _    AUX     VBD   Tense=Past|Mood=Ind|VerbForm=Fin|Person=3  _        3    aux      _   _
5   be          _    AUX     VBG   VerbForm=Ger        _        3    aux_pass             _   _
6   head        _    NOUN    NN    Number=Sing         _        3    obl      _   _
7   .           _    PUNCT   .     _        _        3    punct    _   _
8   by          _    ADP     IN    _        _        6    case     _   _
9   the         _    DET     DT    Definite=Def|PronType=Art          _        6    det      _   _
10  firm        _    NOUN    NN    Number=Sing         _        6    nmod     _   _
11  a           _    DET     DT    Definite=Ind|PronType=Art          _        10   det      _   _
12  investment       _    NOUN    NN         Number=Sing         _        10   compound         _   _
13  of          _    ADP     IN    _        _        10   case     _   _
```

Figure 2: Shallow input (Track 1) derived from UD structure in Figure 1.

```
1   third       _    ADJ     _    Degree=Pos          _        2    A2       _   _
2   run         _    VERB    _    Tense=Past|Aspect=Progr       _        0    ROOT     _   _
3   head        _    NOUN    _    Number=Sing|Definiteness=Def       _        2    A1       _   _
4   firm        _    NOUN    _    Number=Sing|Definiteness=Indef     _        3    A2       _   _
5   investment       _    NOUN    _         Number=Sing         _        4    AM       _   _
```

Figure 3: Deep input (Track 2) derived from UD structure in Figure 1.

node for the subject is added if an originally finite verb has no first argument and no available argument to build a passive; for a pro-drop language such as Spanish, a dummy pronoun is added if the first argument is missing.

7. Surface-level morphologically relevant information as prescribed by syntactic structure or agreement (such as verbal finiteness or verbal number) is removed, whereas semantic-level information such as nominal number and verbal tense is retained.

8. Fine-grained PoS labels found in some treebanks (see e.g. column 5 in Figure 2) are removed, and only coarse-grained ones are retained (column 4 in Figures 2 and 3).

Shallow Track inputs were generated with the aid of a simple Python script from the original UD structures. During the conversion, we filtered out sentences that contained dependencies that only make sense in an analysis context (e.g. *reparandum*, or *orphan*). This amounted to around 1.5% of sentences for the different languages on average; see Table 2 for an overview of the final sizes of the datasets. Deep Track inputs were

then generated by automatically processing the Shallow Track structures using a series of graph-transduction grammars that cover steps 3–8 above (in a similar fashion as Mille et al. (2017)). There is a node-to-node correspondence between the deep and shallow input structures.

The Deep Track inputs can be seen as closer to a realistic application context for NLG systems, in which the component that generates the inputs presumably would not have access to syntactic or language-specific information (see, e.g. the inputs in the SemEval, WebNLG, E2E shared tasks). At the same time, we used only information found in the UD syntactic structures to create the deep inputs, and tried to keep their structure simple. It can be argued that not all the information necessary to reconstruct the original sentences is available in the Deep Track inputs. Task definitions specifically designed for NLG, as used e.g. in SemEval Task 9, tend to use abstract meaning representations (AMRs) as inputs that contain additional information such as OntoNotes labelling or typed circumstantials, which make the generation task easier. In the SR'18 Deep Track inputs, words are not disambiguated, full prepositions may be missing, and some argument relations may be underspecified or missing.

Deep label	Description	Example
A1, A2, ..., A6	nth argument of a predicate	fall→ the ball
A1INV, ..., A6INV	nth inverted argument of a predicate	the ball→ fall
AM/AMINV	(i) none of governor or dependent are argument of the other (ii) unknown argument slot	fall→ last night
LIST	List of elements	fall→ [and] bounce
NAME	Part of a name	Tower→ Eiffel
DEP	Undefined dependent	N/A

Table 1: Deep labels.

	ar	cs	en	es	fi	fr	it	nl	pt	ru
train	6,016	66,485	12,318	12,375	12,030	14,529	12,796	8,325	48,119	14,289
dev	897	9,016	1,978	1,651	1,336	1,473	562	720	559	6,441
test	676	9,876	685	2,061	1,525	416	480	476	6,366	1,719

Table 2: SR'18 dataset sizes for training, development and test sets.

3 Evaluation Methods

3.1 Automatic methods

We used BLEU, NIST, and inverse normalised character-based string-edit distance (referred to as DIST, for short, below) to assess submitted systems. BLEU (Papineni et al., 2002) is a precision metric that computes the geometric mean of the n-gram precisions between generated text and reference texts and adds a brevity penalty for shorter sentences. We use the smoothed version and report results for $n = 4$.

NIST[9] is a related n-gram similarity metric weighted in favour of less frequent n-grams which are taken to be more informative.

Inverse, normalised, character-based string-edit distance (DIST in the tables below) starts by computing the minimum number of character inserts, deletes and substitutions (all at cost 1) required to turn the system output into the (single) reference text. The resulting number is then divided by the number of characters in the reference text, and finally subtracted from 1, in order to align with the other metrics. Spaces and punctuation marks count as characters; output texts were otherwise normalised as for all metrics (see below).

The figures in the tables below are the system-level scores for BLEU and NIST, and the mean sentence-level scores for DIST.

Text normalisation: Output texts were normalised prior to computing metrics by lower-casing all tokens, removing any extraneous whitespace characters.

---

[9]http://www.itl.nist.gov/iad/mig/tests/mt/doc/ngram-study.pdf; http://www.itl.nist.gov/iad/mig/tests/mt/2009/

Missing outputs: Missing outputs were scored 0. Since coverage was 100% for all systems except one, we only report results for all sentences (incorporating the missing-output penalty), rather than also separately reporting scores for just the in-coverage items.

3.2 Human-assessed methods

We assessed two quality criteria in the human evaluations, in separate evaluation experiments: *Readability* and *Meaning Similarity*. As in SR'11 (Belz et al., 2011), we used continuous sliders as rating tools, because raters tend to prefer them (Belz and Kow, 2011). Slider positions were mapped to values from 0 to 100 (best). Raters were first given brief instructions, including instructions to ignore formatting errors, superfluous whitespace, capitalisation issues, and poor hyphenation. The part of the instructions used only in the Readability assessment experiments was:

> "The quality criterion you need to assess is Readability. This is sometimes called fluency, and your task is to decide how well the given text reads; is it good fluent English, or does it have grammatical errors, awkward constructions, etc.
>
> Please rate the text by moving the slider to the position that corresponds to your rating, where 0 is the worst, and 100 is the best rating."

The corresponding instructions for Meaning Similarity assessment, in which system outputs were compared to reference sentences, were as follows:

> "The quality criterion you need to assess is Meaning Similarity. You need to read

both texts, and then decide how close in meaning the second text (in black) is to the first (in grey).

Please use the slider at the bottom of the page to express your rating. The closer in meaning the second text clipping is to the first, the further to the right (towards 100) you need to place the slider.

In other words, a rating of 100% would mean that the meaning of the two text clippings is exactly identical."

Slider design: In SR'11, a slider design was used, which had a smiley face at the 100 end and a frowning face at the 0 end, with the pointer starting out at 50. For conformity with what has emerged as a new affordable human evaluation standard over the past two years in the main machine translation shared tasks held at WMT (Bojar et al., 2017a), we changed this design to look as follows, with the pointer starting at 0:

0 %   100 %

Test data sets for human evaluations: Test set sizes out of the box varied considerably for the different languages. For the human test sets we selected either the entire set or a subset of 1,000, whichever was the smaller number, for a given language. For subsets, test set items were selected randomly but ensuring a similar sentence length distribution as in the whole set.

Reported scores: Again in keeping with the WMT approach, we report both average raw scores and average standardised scores per system. In order to produce standardised scores we simply map each individual evaluator's scores to their standard scores (or z-scores) computed on the set of all raw scores by the given evaluator using each evaluator's mean and standard deviation. For both raw and standard scores, we compute the mean of sentence-level scores.

3.2.1 Mechanical Turk evaluations

For three of the languages in the shallow track (English, Spanish and French), we replicated the human evaluation method from WMT'17, known as Direct Assessment (DA) (Graham et al., 2016), exactly, except that we also ran (separate) experiments to assess the Readability criterion, using the same method.

Quality assurance: System outputs are randomly assigned to HITs (following Mechanical Turk terminology) of 100 outputs, of which 20 are used solely for quality assurance (QA) (i.e. do not count towards system scores): (i) some are repeated as are, (ii) some are repeated in a 'damaged' version and (iii) some are replaced by their corresponding reference texts. In each case, a minimum threshold has to be reached for the HIT to be accepted: for (i), scores must be similar enough, for (ii) the score for the damaged version must be worse, and for (iii) the score for the reference text must be high. For full details of how these additional texts are created and thresholds applied, please refer to Bojar et al. (2017a). Below we report QA figures for the MTurk evaluations (Section 3.2.1).

Code: We were able to reuse, with minor adaptations, the code produced for the WMT'17 evaluations.[10]

3.2.2 Google Data Compute Evaluation

In order to cover more languages, and to enable comparison between crowdsourced and expert evaluation, we also conducted human evaluations using Google's internal 'Data Compute' system evaluation service, where experienced evaluators carefully assess each system output. We used an interface that matches the WMT'17 interface above, as closely as was possible within the constraints of the Data Compute platform.

Everything stated at the beginning of Section 3.2 also holds for the expert annotator evaluations with Google Data Compute.

Quality assurance: Because in the Google Data Compute version of the evaluation experiment we were using expert evaluators from a pool of workers routinely employed to perform such tasks, we did not replicate the WMT'17 QA techniques precisely, opting for a simpler test of self-consistency, or intra-evaluator agreement (IEA) instead. Test set items were randomly grouped into sets of 100 (which we are also calling HITs here for uniformity) and order was again randomised before presentation to evaluators. Each evaluator did at least one HIT. Each HIT contained 5 items which were duplicated to test for IEA which we computed as the average Pearson correlation coefficient per HIT. The average IEA for English was 0.75 on the

---

[10]https://github.com/ygraham/segment-mteval

raw scores for Meaning Similarity, and 0.66 for Readability.

4 Overview of Submitted Systems

Eight different teams (out of twenty-one registered) submitted outputs to SR'18: the ADAPT Centre (ADAPT, Ireland), AX Semantics (AX, Germany), IIT-BHU Varanasi (IIT-BHU, India), Ohio State University (OSU, USA), University of São Paulo (NILC, Brazil), Tilburg University (Tilburg, The Netherlands), Università degli Studi di Torino (DipInfo-UniTo, Italy), and Technische Universität Darmstadt (BinLin, Germany).

All teams submitted outputs for at least the English Shallow Track; one team participated in the Deep Track (ADAPT, English), and three teams submitted outputs for all ten languages of the Shallow Track (AX, OSU, and BinLin). Most submitted systems are based on neural components, and break down the surface realisation task into two subtasks: linearisation, and word inflection. Details of each approach are provided in the teams' reports elsewhere in this volume; here, we briefly summarise each approach:

ADAPT uses linearised parse tree inputs to train a sequence-to-sequence LSTM model with copy attention, augmenting the training set with additional synthetic data.

AX is trained on word pairs for ordering and is combined with a rule-based morphology component.

IIT-BHU uses an LSTM-based encoder-decoder model for word re-inflection, and a Language Model-based approach for word reordering.

OSU first generates inflected wordforms with a neural sequence-to-sequence model, and then incrementally linearises them using a global linear model over features that take into account the dependency structure and dependency location.[11]

NILC is a neural-based system that uses a bottom-up approach to build the sentence using the dependency relations together with a language model, and language-specific lexicons to produce the word forms of each lemma in the sentence.

Tilburg works by first preprocessing an input dependency tree into an ordered linearised string,

which is then realised using a statistical machine translation model.

DipInfo-UniTo employs two separate neural networks with different architectures to predict the word ordering and the morphological inflection independently; outputs are combined to produce the final sentence.

BinLin uses one neural module as a binary classifier in a sequential process of ordering token lemmas, and another for character-level morphology generation where the words are inflected to finish the surface realisation.

5 Evaluation results

5.1 Results from metric evaluations

Tables 3–5 show BLEU-4, NIST, and DIST results for both the Shallow and Deep tracks, for all submitted systems; results are listed in order of number of languages submitted for. Best results for each language are shown in boldface.

In terms of BLEU-4, in the Shallow Track, Tilburg obtained the best scores for four languages (French, Italian, Dutch, Portuguese), OSU for three (Arabic, Spanish, Finnish), BinLin for two (Czech, Russian), and ADAPT for one (English). The highest BLEU-4 scores across languages were obtained on the English and Spanish datasets, with BLEU-4 scores of 69.14 (ADAPT) and 65.31 (OSU) respectively.

Results are identical for DIST, except that AX, rather than BinLin, has the highest score for Czech. The picture for NIST is also very similar to that for BLEU-4, except that ADAPT and OSU are tied for best NIST score for English, and BinLin (rather than Tilburg) has the best NIST score for Dutch.

In the Deep Track, only ADAPT submitted system outputs (English), and as expected, the scores are much lower than for the Shallow Track, across all metrics.

5.2 Results from human evaluations

Given the small number of submissions in the Deep Track, we conducted human evaluations for the Shallow Track only. We used Mechanical Turk for the three languages for which this is feasible (English, Spanish and French), and our aim was to also conduct evaluations via Google's Data Compute service for three additional languages which had the next highest numbers of submissions, as

---

[11] Some of OSU's outputs were submitted after the start of the human evaluations and are not included in this report; outputs submitted late, but before the human evaluation started, are included and marked with asterisks in the results tables.

	Shallow										Deep
	ar	cs	en	es	fi	fr	it	nl	pt	ru	en
AX	4.57	9.75	28.09	10.2	7.95	7.87	16.35	14.21	16.29	15.59	–
BinLin	16.2	**25.05**	29.6	32.15	23.26	20.53	23.55	22.69	24.59	**34.34**	–
OSU	**25.65***	–	66.33	**65.31**	**37.52***	38.24*	–	25.52*	–	–	–
Tilburg	–	–	55.29	49.47	–	**52.03**	**44.46**	**32.28**	**30.82**	–	–
DipInfo	–	–	23.2	26.9	–	23.12	24.61	–	–	–	–
NILC	–	–	50.74	51.58	–	–	–	–	27.12	–	–
ADAPT	–	–	**69.14**	–	–	–	–	–	–	–	**21.67**
IIT-BHU	–	–	8.04	–	–	–	–	–	–	–	–

Table 3: BLEU-4 scores for the test data. Bold = best score per language. * = late submission.

	Shallow										Deep
	ar	cs	en	es	fi	fr	it	nl	pt	ru	en
AX	5.13	9.33	9.51	8.26	6.84	6.45	6.83	7.81	6.78	9.93	–
BinLin	6.94	**10.74**	9.58	10.21	9.36	7.21	7.6	**8.64**	7.54	**13.06**	–
OSU	**7.15***	–	**12.02**	**12.74**	**9.56***	8.00*	–	7.33*	–	–	–
Tilburg	–	–	10.86	11.12	–	**9.85**	**9.11**	8.05	**7.55**	–	–
DipInfo	–	–	8.86	9.58	–	7.72	8.25	–	–	–	–
NILC	–	–	10.62	11.17	–	–	–	–	7.56	–	–
ADAPT	–	–	**12.02**	–	–	–	–	–	–	–	6.95
IIT-BHU	–	–	7.71	–	–	–	–	–	–	–	–

Table 4: NIST scores for the test data. Bold = best score per language. * = late submission.

	Shallow										Deep
	ar	cs	en	es	fi	fr	it	nl	pt	ru	en
AX	38.96	**36.48**	70.01	21.12	35.59	22.3	40.96	49.65	51.7	34.28	–
BinLin	44.37	35.7	65.9	36.95	41.21	28.6	40.74	48.23	51.36	**34.56**	–
OSU	**46.49***	–	70.22	**61.46**	**58.7***	53.69*	–	57.77*	–	–	–
Tilburg	–	–	79.29	51.73	–	**55.54**	**58.61**	**57.81**	**60.7**	–	–
DipInfo	–	–	51.87	24.53	–	18.04	36.11	–	–	–	–
NILC	–	–	77.56	53.78	–	–	–	–	57.43	–	–
ADAPT	–	–	**80.42**	–	–	–	–	–	–	–	48.69
IIT-BHU	–	–	47.63	–	–	–	–	–	–	–	–

Table 5: DIST scores for the test data. Bold = best score per language. * = late submission.

well as for English in order to enable us to compare results obtained with the two different methods. However, most of the latter evaluations are still ongoing and will be reported separately in a future paper. Below, we report Google Data Compute results and comparisons with Mechanical Turk results, for English only.

5.2.1 Mechanical Turk results

Tables 6, 7 and 8 show the results of the human evaluation carried out via Mechanical Turk with Direct Assessment (MTurk DA), for English, French and Spanish, respectively. See Section 3.2 for details of the evaluation method. 'DA' refers to the specific way in which scores are collected in the WMT approach which differs from what we did for SR'11, and here in the Google Data Compute experiments.

English: Average Meaning Similarity DA scores for English systems range from 86.9% to 67% with OSU achieving the highest overall score in terms of both average raw DA scores and corresponding z-scores. Readability scores for the same set of systems range from 78.7% to 41.3%, revealing that MTurk workers rate the Meaning Similarity between generated texts and corresponding reference sentences higher in general than Readability. In order to investigate how Readability of system outputs compare to human-produced text, we included the original test sentences as a system in the Readability evaluation (for Meaning Similarity the notional score is 100%). Unsurprisingly, human text achieves the highest score in terms of Readability (78.7%) but is quite closely followed by the best performing system in terms of Readability, ADAPT (73.9%).

Overall in the English Shallow Track, average DA scores for systems are close. We tested for statistical significance of differences between average DA scores using a Wilcoxon rank sum test.

Figure 4 shows significance test results for each pair of systems participating in the English evaluation in the form of heatmaps where a green cell denotes a significantly higher average score for the system in that row over the system in that column, with a darker shade of green denoting a conclusion drawn with more certainty. Results show that two entries are tied for first place in terms of Meaning Similarity, OSU and ADAPT, with the small difference in average scores proving not statistically significant. In terms of Readability, however, the ADAPT sentences achieve a significantly higher readability score compared to OSU.

French: Table 7 shows average DA scores for systems participating in the French Shallow Track. Meaning Similarity scores for French systems range from 72.9% to 48.6% with the Tilburg system achieving the highest overall score. In terms of Readability, again Tilburg achieves the highest average score of 65.4%, with a considerable gap to the next best entry, OSU. Compared to the human results, there is a larger gap than we saw for English outputs.

Figure 5 shows results of tests for statistical significance between average DA scores for systems in the French Shallow Track. Tilburg achieves a significantly higher average DA score compared to all other systems in terms of both Meaning Similarity and Readability. All systems are significantly worse in terms of Readability than the human authored texts.

Spanish: Table 8 shows average DA scores for systems participating in the Shallow Track for Spanish. Meaning Similarity scores range from 77.3% to 43.9%, with OSU achieving the highest score. In terms of Readability, the text produced by the systems ranges from 77.0% to 33.0%, and again OSU achieves the highest score. Figure 6 shows results of the corresponding significance tests: OSU significantly outperforms all other participating systems with respect to both evaluation criteria. Human-generated texts are significantly more readable than all system outputs.

MTurk DA quality control: Only 31% of workers passed quality control (being able to replicate scores for same sentences and scoring damaged sentences lower, for full details see Bojar et al., 2017a), highlighting the danger of crowdsourcing without good quality control measures. The remaining 69%, who did not meet this criterion, were omitted from computation of the official DA results above. Of those 31% included in the evaluation, a very high proportion, 97%, showed no significant difference in scores collected in repeated assessment of the same sentences; these high levels of agreement are consistent with what we have seen in DA used for Machine Translation (Graham et al., 2016) and Video Captioning evaluation (Graham et al., 2017).

Agreement with automatic metrics: Table 9 shows Pearson correlations between MTurk DA scores and automatic metric scores in the English, French and Spanish shallow tracks. Overall, BLEU agrees most consistently across the different tasks, achieving a correlation above 0.95 in all settings, whereas the correlation of NIST scores with human Meaning Similarity scores is just 0.854 for French, while DIST scores correlate with human Readability scores at just 0.831 for English.

Conclusions from metric correlations should be drawn with a degree of caution, since in all cases the sample size from which we compute correlations is small, 8 systems for English, 5 for French, and 6 for Spanish. We carried out significance tests to investigate to what degree differences in correlations are likely to occur by chance. In order to take into account the fact that we are comparing correlations between human assessment and competing pairs of metrics (where metric scores themselves correlate with each other), we apply a Williams test for significance of differences in *dependent* correlations, as done in evaluation of Machine Translation metrics (Graham and Baldwin, 2014; Bojar et al., 2017b).

Results are shown in Table 9. Correlations between metrics and human assessment in bold are *not* significantly lower than any other metric. As can be seen from Table 9, there is no significant difference between any of the three metrics in terms of correlation with human assessment in both the French and Spanish tracks. In the English track, however, the correlation of BLEU and NIST scores with human assessment are significantly higher than that of DIST.

5.2.2 Google Data Compute results

Table 10 shows the results for the English assessment conducted via the Google Data Compute (GDC) evaluation service with expert evaluators.

One difference between the MTurk and the Google results is the range of scores, which for

	Meaning Similarity					Readability			
%	z	n	Assess.	System	%	z	n	Assess.	System
					78.7	0.797	831	1,350	HUMAN
86.9	0.369	1,249	1,422	OSU	73.9	0.638	1,065	1,301	ADAPT
85.5	0.314	1,238	1,429	ADAPT	71.2	0.558	1,117	1,374	OSU
84.8	0.291	1,294	1,498	Tilburg	62.1	0.258	1,109	1,377	Tilburg
84.2	0.280	1,229	1,407	NILC	58.1	0.166	1,086	1,342	NILC
77.5	0.043	1,256	1,442	AX	52.5	−0.019	1,080	1,343	AX
75.8	0	1,264	1,462	BinLin	50.1	−0.102	1,076	1,336	BinLin
72.6	−0.120	1,244	1,427	DipInfo	42.7	−0.345	1,091	1,355	DipInfo
67.0	−0.312	1,257	1,412	IIT-BHU	41.3	−0.376	1,081	1,296	IIT-BHU

Table 6: MTurk DA human evaluation results for English Shallow Track; % = average DA score (0-100); z = z-score; n = number of distinct sentences assessed; Assess. = total number of sentences assessed.

	Meaning Similarity					Readability			
%	z	n	Assess.	System	%	z	n	Assess.	System
					89.9	1.525	218	650	HUMAN
72.9	0.365	416	1,651	Tilburg	65.4	0.607	416	1060	Tilburg
69.1	0.237	416	1,570	OSU	54.7	0.179	416	1007	OSU
58.9	−0.133	416	1,575	BinLin	41.5	−0.26	416	1031	BinLin
52.8	−0.32	416	1,648	DipInfo	38.7	0.456	416	1094	DipInfo
48.6	−0.444	416	1,592	AX	32.9	−0.659	416	1033	AX

Table 7: MTurk DA human evaluation results for French Shallow Track; % = average DA score (0-100); z = z-score; n = number of distinct sentences assessed; Assess. = total number of sentences assessed.

	Meaning Similarity					Readability			
%	z	n	Assess.	System	DA	z	n	Assess.	System
					89.6	1.120	889	1,237	HUMAN
77.3	0.519	1,255	1,502	OSU	77.0	0.731	1,399	1,691	OSU
66.8	0.175	1,231	1,439	NILC	63.1	0.265	1,371	1,645	Tilburg
65.7	0.136	1,190	1,401	Tilburg	57.2	0.093	1,384	1,631	NILC
54.9	−0.214	1,202	1,395	BinLin	45.1	−0.299	1,367	1,625	BinLin
48.4	−0.445	1,190	1,401	DipInfo	36.9	−0.558	1,370	1,629	DipInfo
43.9	−0.583	1,225	1,449	AX	33.0	−0.700	1,371	1,657	AX

Table 8: MTurk DA human evaluation results for Spanish Shallow Track; % = average DA score (0-100); z = z-score; n = number of distinct sentences assessed; Assess. = total number of sentences assessed.

		Meaning Sim.	BLEU	NIST	DIST
English	Meaning Sim.		**0.968**	**0.967**	0.911
	Readability	0.927	**0.971**	**0.977**	0.831
French	Meaning Sim.		**0.954**	0.854	**0.968**
	Readability	0.984	**0.978**	**0.924**	**0.938**
Spanish	Meaning Sim.		**0.986**	**0.980**	**0.990**
	Readability	0.989	**0.969**	**0.971**	**0.969**

Table 9: Pearson correlation of DA human evaluation scores with Automatic Metrics for English, French and Spanish Shallow Track.

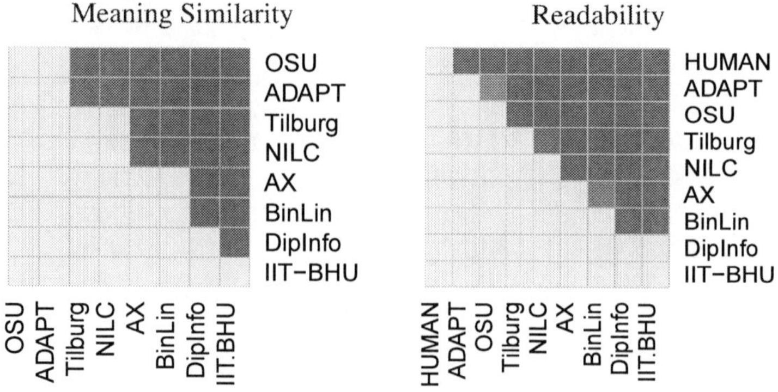

Figure 4: MTurk DA human evaluation significance test results for the English shallow track.

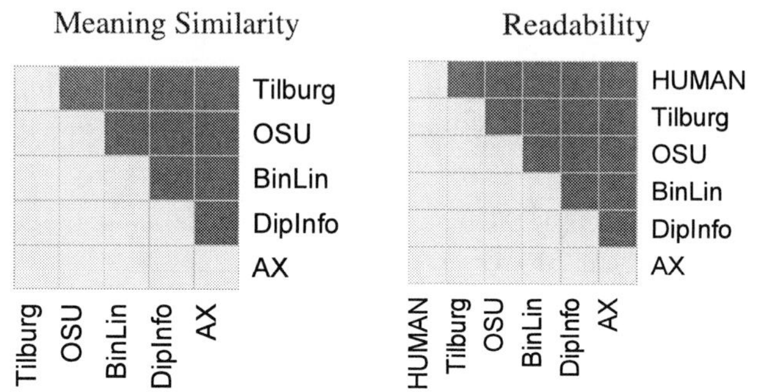

Figure 5: MTurk DA human evaluation significance test results for the French shallow track.

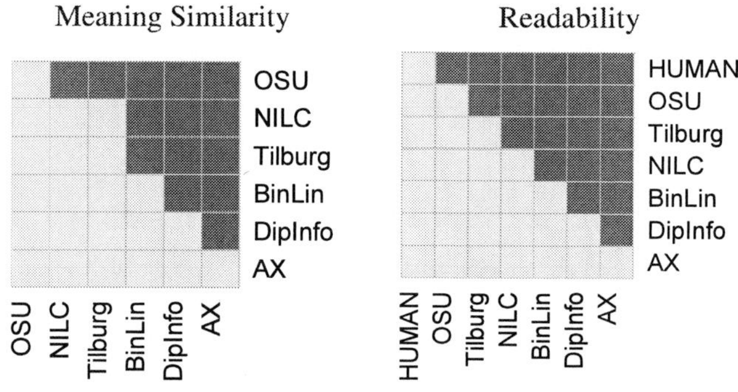

Figure 6: MTurk DA human evaluation significance test results for the Spanish shallow track.

Meaning Similarity range from 67 to 86.9 for MTurk, compared to 52 to 86.1 for GDC. The latter is a wider range of scores, and expert evaluators' scores distinguish between systems more clearly than the crowdsourced scores which place the top four systems very close together.

Readability scores range from 41.3 to 78.7 for MTurk, and from 60.2 to 88.2 for GDC. The expert evaluators tended to assign higher scores overall, but their range and the way they distinguish between systems is similar. For example, neither evaluation found much difference for the bottom two systems.

The rank order of systems in the two separate evaluations is identical. Table 11 shows the Pearson correlation of scores for systems in the evaluations, where meaning similarity scores correlate almost perfectly at 0.997 (raw %) and 0.993 (z) and readability at 0.986 (raw %) and 0.985 (z).

6 Conclusion

SR'18 was the second surface realisation shared task, and followed an earlier pilot task for English, SR'11. Participation was high for a first instance

Meaning Similarity				Readability			
%	z	n	System	%	z	n	System
86.1	0.479	1000	OSU	88.2	0.530	1000	ADAPT
83.8	0.394	1000	ADAPT	86.1	0.459	1000	OSU
81.8	0.308	1000	Tilburg	81.0	0.276	1000	Tilburg
78.8	0.219	1000	NILC	78.0	0.156	1000	NILC
68.7	-0.109	1000	AX	67.7	-0.194	1000	AX
65.4	-0.238	1000	BinLin	65.9	-0.299	1000	BinLin
59.7	-0.414	1000	DipInfo	60.7	-0.449	1000	DipInfo
52.0	-0.640	1000	IIT-BHU	60.2	-0.480	1000	IIT-BHU

Table 10: Google Data Compute human evaluation results for the English shallow track, where % = average score (0-100) for generated sentences; n distinct sentences assessed per system.

	Meaning Similarity	Readability
%	0.997	0.986
z	0.993	0.985

Table 11: Pearson correlation between human evaluations carried out using MTurk DA and Google Data Compute.

of a shared task, at least in the Shallow Track, indicating that interest is high enough to continue running it again next year to enable more teams to participate.

One important question that needs to be addressed is to what extent UDs are suitable inputs for NLG systems. More specifically, can they reasonably be expected to be generated by other, content-determining, modules in an NLG system, do they provide all the information necessary to generate surface realisations, and if not, how can they be augmented to provide it.

We hope to discuss these and related issues with the research community as we prepare the next instance of the SR Task. A goal to aim for may be to make it possible for different NLG components to be connected via standard interface representations, to increase re-usability for NLG components. However, what may constitute a good interface representation for surface realisation remains far from clear.

Acknowledgments

The work reported in this paper has been partly supported by Science Foundation Ireland (sfi.ie) under the SFI Research Centres Programme co-funded under the European Regional Development Fund, grant number 13/RC/2106 (ADAPT Centre for Digital Content Technology, www.adaptcentre.ie) at Dublin City University, and by the European Commission in the framework of the H2020 Programme under the contract numbers 779962-RIA, 700475-IA, 7000024-RIA, and 645012RIA.

References

Anja Belz and Eric Kow. 2011. Discrete vs. continuous rating scales for language evaluation in NLP. In *Proceedings of the 49th Annual Meeting of the Association for Computational Linguistics (ACL-HLT'11)*.

Anja Belz, Michael White, Dominic Espinosa, Eric Kow, Deirdre Hogan, and Amanda Stent. 2011. The first surface realisation shared task: Overview and evaluation results. In *Proceedings of the 13th European Workshop on Natural Language Generation*, ENLG '11, pages 217–226, Stroudsburg, PA, USA. Association for Computational Linguistics.

Ondřej Bojar, Rajen Chatterjee, Christian Federmann, Yvette Graham, Barry Haddow, Shujian Huang, Matthias Huck, Philipp Koehn, Qun Liu, Varvara Logacheva, Christof Monz, Matteo Negri, Matt Post, Raphael Rubino, Lucia Specia, and Marco Turchi. 2017a. Findings of the 2017 conference on machine translation (WMT'17). In *Proceedings of the Second Conference on Machine Translation, Volume 2: Shared Task Papers*, pages 169–214, Copenhagen, Denmark. Association for Computational Linguistics.

Ondřej Bojar, Yvette Graham, and Amir Kamran. 2017b. Results of the wmt17 metrics shared task. In *Proceedings of the Second Conference on Machine Translation, Volume 2: Shared Task Papers*, pages 489–513, Copenhagen, Denmark. Association for Computational Linguistics.

Claire Gardent, Anastasia Shimorina, Shashi Narayan, and Laura Perez-Beltrachini. 2017. Creating training corpora for micro-planners. In *Proceedings of the 55th Annual Meeting of the Association for Computational Linguistics (Volume 1: Long Papers)*, Vancouver, Canada. Association for Computational Linguistics.

Yvette Graham, George Awad, and Alan Smeaton. 2017. Evaluation of Automatic Video Captioning Using Direct Assessment. *ArXiv e-prints*.

Yvette Graham and Timothy Baldwin. 2014. Testing for significance of increased correlation with human judgment. In *Proceedings of the 2014 Conference on Empirical Methods in Natural Language Processing (EMNLP)*, pages 172–176, Doha, Qatar. Association for Computational Linguistics.

Yvette Graham, Timothy Baldwin, Alistair Moffat, and Justin Zobel. 2016. Can machine translation systems be evaluated by the crowd alone. *Natural Language Engineering*, FirstView:1–28.

Jonathan May and Jay Priyadarshi. 2017. Semeval-2017 task 9: Abstract meaning representation parsing and generation. In *Proceedings of the 11th International Workshop on Semantic Evaluation (SemEval-2017)*, pages 534–543, Vancouver, Canada. Association for Computational Linguistics.

Adam Meyers, R. Reeves, C. Macleod, R. Szekely, V. Zielinska, B. Young, and R. Grishman. 2004. The NomBank project: An interim report. In *HLT-NAACL 2004 Workshop: Frontiers in Corpus Annotation, Boston, MA, May 2004*, pages 24–31.

Simon Mille, Roberto Carlini, Ivan Latorre, and Leo Wanner. 2017. Upf at epe 2017: Transduction-based deep analysis. In *Shared Task on Extrinsic Parser Evaluation (EPE 2017)*, pages 80–88, Pisa, Italy.

Joakim Nivre and Marie-Catherine de Marneffe et al. 2016. Universal dependencies v1: A multilingual treebank collection. In *Proceedings of LREC*, Portorož, Slovenia.

Jekaterina Novikova, Ondrej Dušek, and Verena Rieser. 2017. The E2E dataset: New challenges for end-to-end generation. In *Proceedings of the 18th Annual Meeting of the Special Interest Group on Discourse and Dialogue*, Saarbrücken, Germany. ArXiv:1706.09254.

Martha Palmer, Daniel Gildea, and Paul Kingsbury. 2005. The proposition bank: An annotated corpus of semantic roles. *Computational Linguistics*, 31(1):71–105.

K. Papineni, S. Roukos, T. Ward, and W. j. Zhu. 2002. BLEU: A method for automatic evaluation of machine translation. In *Proc. 40th Annual Meeting on Association for Computational Linguistics*, pages 311–318, Philadelphia, Pennsylvania.

BinLin: A Simple Method of Dependency Tree Linearization

Yevgeniy Puzikov and **Iryna Gurevych**
Ubiquitous Knowledge Processing Lab (UKP-TUDA)
Department of Computer Science, Technische Universität Darmstadt
Research Training Group AIPHES
{puzikov,gurevych}@ukp.informatik.tu-darmstadt.de

Abstract

Surface Realization Shared Task 2018 is a workshop on generating sentences from lemmatized sets of dependency triples. This paper describes the results of our participation in the challenge. We develop a data-driven pipeline system which first orders the lemmas and then conjugates the words to finish the surface realization process. Our contribution is a novel sequential method of ordering lemmas, which, despite its simplicity, achieves promising results. We demonstrate the effectiveness of the proposed approach, describe its limitations and outline ways to improve it.

1 Introduction

Natural Language generation (NLG) is the task of generating natural language utterances from textual inputs or structured data representations. For many years one of the research foci in the NLG community has been Surface Realization (SR) – the process of transforming a sentence plan into a linearly-ordered, grammatical string of morphologically inflected words (Langkilde-Geary, 2002).

The SR Shared Task is aimed at developing a common input representation that could be used by a variety of NLG systems to generate realizations from (Belz et al., 2011). In the case of the Surface Realization Shared Task 2018 (Mille et al., 2018) there are two different representations the contestants can use, depending on the track they participate in:

Shallow Track: unordered dependency trees consisting of lemmatized nodes with part-of-speech (POS) tags and morphological information as found in the Universal Dependencies (UD) annotations (version 2.0).[1]

Deep Track: same as above, but having functional words and morphological features removed.

We participated in the shallow track, and therefore our task was to generate a sentence by ordering the lemmas and inflecting them to the correct surface forms. The outputs of the participating systems are assessed using both automatic and manual evaluation. The former is performed by computing BLEU (Papineni et al., 2002), NIST (Doddington, 2002), CIDEr (Vedantam et al., 2015) scores and normalized string edit distance (EDIST) between the reference sentence and a system output. Manual evaluation is based on preference judgments: third-year undergraduate students from Cambridge, Oxford and Edinburgh rate pairs of candidate outputs (including the target sentence), scoring them for *Clarity*, *Fluency* and *Meaning Similarity*.

The data used for the task is the UD treebanks distributed in the 10-column CoNLL-U format.[2] The data is available for Arabic, Czech, Dutch, English, Finnish, French, Italian, Portuguese, Russian and Spanish. According to the requirements of the Shallow Track, the information on word order was removed by randomized scrambling of the token sequence; the words were also replaced by their lemmas.

Our contribution is a simple method of dependency tree linearization which orders a bag of lemmas based on the available syntactic information. The major limitation of the method is its input order sensitivity; solving this problem is reserved for future work.

Our paper has the following structure. Section 2 describes related work done in the past. Section 3 presents the results of the exploratory data analysis conducted prior to system development. The details of our system architecture are specified in

---

[1] http://universaldependencies.org/

[2] http://universaldependencies.org/format.html

Proceedings of the First Workshop on Multilingual Surface Realisation, pages 13–28
Melbourne, Australia, July 19, 2018. ©2018 Association for Computational Linguistics

Section 4 which is followed by the description of the experimental setup and evaluation (Section 5). Section 6 mentions the limitations of the proposed surface realization method and outlines future work directions.

2   Related Work

As mentioned in Section 1, the task at hand is to generate a sentence by ordering the lemmas and inflecting them to the correct surface forms. Past research work proposed both joint and pipeline solutions for the problem. Taking into consideration the pipeline nature of our system, we separate the related work stage-wise.

2.1   Syntactic Ordering

Given a bag of input words, a syntactic ordering algorithm constructs an output sentence. Prior work explored a range of approaches to syntactic ordering: grammar-based methods (Elhadad and Robin, 1992; Carroll et al., 1999; White et al., 2007), generate-and-rerank approaches (Bangalore and Rambow, 2000; Langkilde-Geary, 2002), tree linearization using probabilistic language models (Guo et al., 2008), inter alia. Depending on how much syntactic information is available as input, the research on syntactic ordering can be categorized into (1) free word ordering, (2) full tree linearization and (3) partial tree linearization (Liu et al., 2015). The setup of the Surface Realization Task corresponds to the full tree linearization case, since the dependency tree information is provided.

Conceptually, the problem of tree linearization is simple. However, given no constraints, the search space is exponential in the number of tokens, which makes exhaustive search intractable. This stimulated the line of research focusing on the development of approximate search methods. Current state-of-the-art (evaluated on the English data only) belongs to the system of Puduppully et al. (2016) who extended the work of Liu et al. (2015) on developing a transition-based generator. The authors treated language generation process as a generalized form of dependency parsing with unordered token sequences, and used a learning and search framework of Zhang and Clark (2011) to keep the decoding process tractable. A similar approach to dependency tree linearization was explored in (Bohnet et al., 2010), who approximated exact decoding with a beam search. Our method of syntactic ordering is also based on search ap-

proximation, but follows a different approach: we use a greedy search strategy, but restrict the scoring procedure to a smaller set of plausible candidate pairs, which speeds up the search procedure and reduces the number of mistakes the system might make.

2.2   Word Inflection

Word inflection in the context of the Surface Realization Task can be defined as the subtask of generating a surface form (*was*) from a given source lemma (*be*) and additional morphological/syntactic attributes (*Number=Sing*, *Person=3*, *Tense=Past*).

Early work proposed to approach the task with finite state transducers (Koskenniemi, 1983; Kaplan and Kay, 1994). While being accurate, these systems require a lot of time and linguistic expertise to construct and maintain. With the advance of machine learning, the community mostly shifted towards data-driven methods of automatic morphological paradigm induction and string transduction as the method of morphological inflection generation (Yarowsky and Wicentowski, 2000; Wicentowski, 2004; Dreyer and Eisner, 2011; Durrett and DeNero, 2013; Ahlberg et al., 2015). In comparison with their rule-based counterparts, these approaches scale better across languages and domains, but require manually-defined comprehensive feature representation of the inputs.

Current research focuses on data-driven models which learn a high-dimensional feature representation of the input data during the optimization procedure in an end-to-end fashion. Recent work (Faruqui et al., 2016) proposed to model the problem as a sequence-to-sequence learning task, using the encoder-decoder neural network architecture developed in the machine translation community (Cho et al., 2014; Sutskever et al., 2014). This approach showed an improvement over conventional machine learning models, but failed to address the issue of poor sample complexity of complex neural networks – in practice, the approach did not perform well on low-resource or morphologically rich languages.

An attempt to address this issue was made by Aharoni and Goldberg (2017), who proposed to directly model an almost monotonic alignment between the input and output character sequences by using a controllable hard attention mechanism which allows the network to jointly align and transduce, while maintaining a focused representation at

Property	Language									
	ar	**cs**	**en**	**es**	**fi**	**fr**	**it**	**nl**	**pt**	**ru**
unique features	37	**112**	36	56	89	35	41	66	48	40
OOV lemmas	1056	**3299**	1180	1368	1598	1895	439	973	535	2723
OOV forms	1745	8070	1313	2131	3666	2387	683	1131	785	**8190**
OOV chars	0	2	3	1	5	**12**	2	0	0	0

Table 1: Cross-lingual data analysis.

each step. The authors proposed to utilize independently learned character-level alignments instead of the weighted sum of representations (as done in the soft attention models). Experimental results demonstrated better sample efficiency of the models trained according to the proposed method, and considerable improvements over the previous approaches.

3 Data Analysis

For the input to the shallow track, the organizers separated the reference sentences from the respective structures. Although the one-to-one correspondence between sentences and dependency trees was preserved, the alignment between the lemmas in the trees and the word forms in the sentences was lost. To circumvent this issue and ease the burden of aligning lemmas with the corresponding surface forms, we decided to use the original UD data files for all our experiments – they contain the same dependency trees as the shared task data, but the order of the tokens is not scrambled and each surface form is aligned with the respective lemma.

Prior to system development, we analyzed the data along the dimensions which we deemed relevant for the task. Due to space constraints here we show figures and numbers mainly for English; the analysis results for other languages can be found in Appendix A.1.

First, we examined the lemma-to-form ratio (Figure 1). The majority of lemmas have only one surface form, which suggests a strong majority baseline for the morphological inflection subtask. However, languages with rich morphology (Czech, Finnish, Russian) pose a challenge in this regard and call for a more elaborate approach which takes into account complex grammar inflection paradigms. The number of unique features (values in the FEAT column of the input data) served as a rough estimate of the latter (Table 1). We have not performed any language-specific engineering to address these linguistic properties, but took them

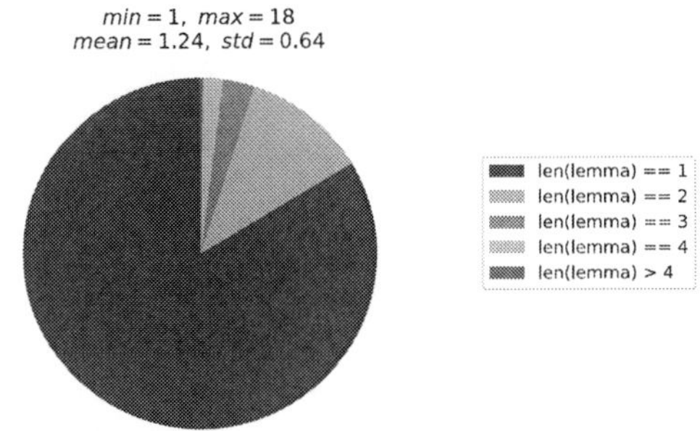

Figure 1: Lemma-to-form ratio (English).

into consideration for future work.

Another important data property is the length distribution of lemmas, surface forms and sentences. We computed the training data statistics and used the obtained estimates to establish cut-off thresholds for filtering out outlier lemmas and forms from the training data.

The number of out-of-vocabulary (OOV) language units can be viewed as a crude measure of the expected difference between training and development data distributions. Table 1 shows the number of OOV lemmas, surface forms and characters for each of the languages. Some of the datasets included foreign names and terms which are used in their original language forms. For example, out of 356464 French data tokens, 419 include characters that are not digits, punctuation signs or letters of the French alphabet. Since such words are usually not conjugated, but copied verbatim, we consider them as outliers and exclude them from the training procedure. Finally, tokens defined in the UD annotation guidelines as multi-word expressions (MWE) and empty nodes were excluded from the training data, because they require language-specific treatment (*e.g.*, the French data includes 9750 tokens which were identified as MWE; out of 870033 tokens in the Russian dataset, 1092 correspond to empty nodes).

When approaching the task of syntactic ordering,

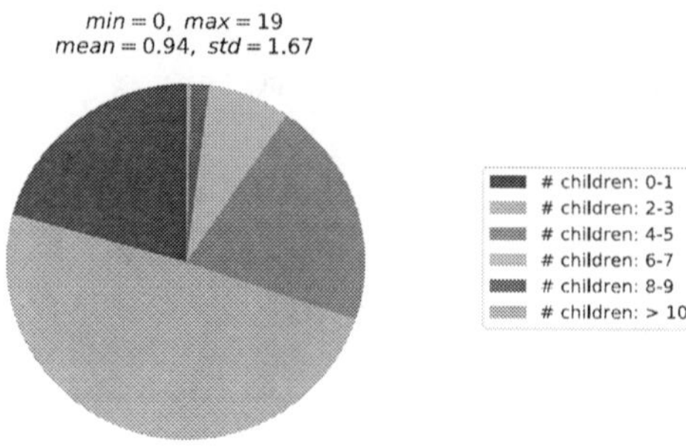

Figure 2: Branching factor of the dependency trees (English).

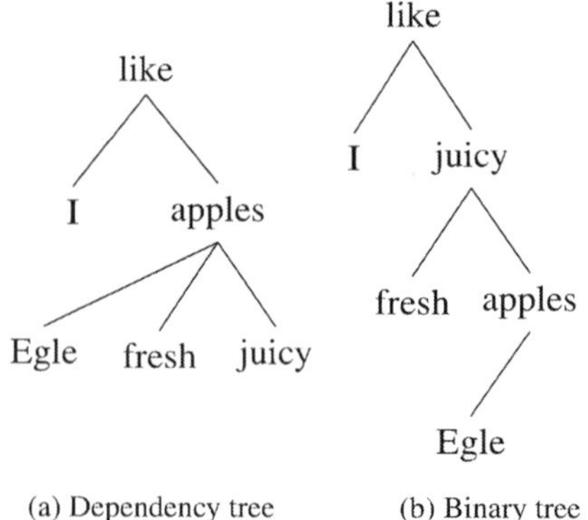

(a) Dependency tree   (b) Binary tree

Figure 3: A dependency tree and a binary tree, constructed according to Algorithm 1. Reference sentence: "I like fresh juicy Egle apples".

one needs to take into account the complexity of the tree structures. We found the branching factor to be very informative in this regard: for each node in each tree we counted the number of children the node has. Most nodes in the dependency trees of all examined languages have one to three children (Figure 2 shows the distribution of branching factor values for English). This solicits decomposition of the syntactic ordering procedure over subtrees, similar to what was done in (He et al., 2009).

4 Our Approach

This section describes the approach we developed for the shared task.

Given a dependency tree, we first decompose it into subtrees each having one head and an arbitrary number of children. Each subtree is being linearized as follows: for each of the children nodes we predict whether it should be positioned to the left or to the right of the head node, and store this positional information in a binary tree structure. We move up the original tree, linearizing subtrees until we reach the root node. At this point we have processed all nodes from the original dependency tree – it can be now completely linearized by traversing the binary tree with the root as a head node.

Since each dependency node is labeled with the corresponding lemma, it is trivial to obtain a lemma sequence from the linearized dependency tree. We further use the morphological inflection generator component to predict a surface form for each lemma in the sequence and in this way generate a sentence.

4.1 Syntactic Component

The first step of the proposed pipeline orders the nodes of the dependency tree into a sequence which ideally mirrors the order of words in the reference sentence. The main difficulty of this step is finding a sorting or ranking method which avoids making many node comparisons or scoring decisions. We propose an ordering procedure which uses a given dependency tree and constructs a binary tree storing the original dependency nodes (lemmas) in a sorted order (Algorithm 1) .

As input, the algorithm takes a dependency tree and a classifier trained to make binary decisions of positioning child nodes to the right/left of the head node. First, we decompose the tree into local subtrees, represented by *(head, children)* node groups. This is achieved by running a breadth-first search (BFS) algorithm on the input dependency tree (line 4 of the pseudocode). For each *(head, children)* group, we further apply the following steps:

- initialize a binary tree with the head node (line 5)

- iterate over the child nodes and use the classifier to predict whether the child should be inserted to the left or to the right of the head node (lines 6-7)

When the binary tree construction is finished, we can obtain a sorted lemma sequence by performing in-order traversal on the resulting binary tree.

The core of the procedure is the insertion of a new node into the binary tree (Algorithm 2). Given a node pair (n_i, n_j), a classifier is used to predict whether n_j should be positioned to the left or to

Algorithm 1: Given a dependency tree dg and a binary classifier clf, construct a binary tree and traverse it to order dependency nodes. BFS denotes the breadth-first search procedure.

```
1: function ORDERNODES(clf, dg)
2:    root ← dg.root
3:    decisions ← {}
4:    for head, children ∈ BFS(dg) do
5:       bt ← BinTree(head)
6:       for child ∈ children do
7:          InsertNode(bt, child, clf)
8:       end for
9:       decisions[head] = Traverse(bt)
10:   end for
11:   order = OrderDec(root, decisions)
12:   return order
13: end function
```

the right of n_i. The decision is made based on the feature representation of the two nodes.

Algorithm 2: A recursive procedure of inserting a new node $child$ into a binary tree bt, using a binary classifier clf.

```
1: procedure INSERTNODE(bt, child, clf)
2:    bf ← GetFeat(bt)
3:    cf ← GetFeat(child)
4:    label ← MakeDecision(clf, cf, bf)
5:    if label is LEFT then
6:       if bt.left is None then
7:          bt.left ← BinTree(child)
8:       else
9:          InsertNode(bt.left, child, clf)
10:      end if
11:   else
12:      if bt.right is None then
13:         bt.right ← BinTree(child)
14:      else
15:         InsertNode(bt.right, child, clf)
16:      end if
17:   end if
18: end procedure
```

For simplicity, we decided to use a multi-layer perceptron as a classifier (Figure 4).

Given a pair of nodes (n_i, n_j), we first extract their features. We consider the node itself, it's head and one (any) child in the dependency tree as the neighborhood elements and extract the corresponding lemmas, POS-tags (both XPOS and UPOS), and dependency edge labels. Thus, the feature set

$$(4)\ o = sigm(\mathbf{h}_2)$$

$$(3)\ \mathbf{h}_2 = lrelu(\mathbf{W}_2 \mathbf{h}_1)$$

$$(2)\ \mathbf{h}_1 = \mathbf{W}_1 \mathbf{x}$$

$$(1)\ \mathbf{x} = [\mathbf{n}_j^e; \mathbf{n}_i^e]$$

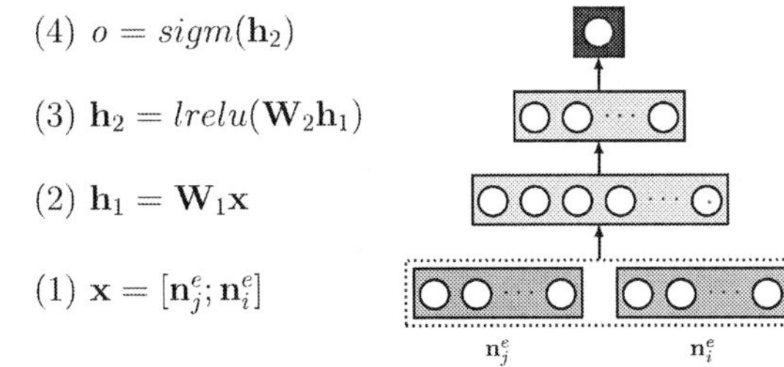

Figure 4: Schematic view of the neural network architecture used as a classifier in the syntactic ordering component of our system.

for one node in the node pair consists of $N = 3$ (neighborhood elements) $\times$ 4 (features) $= 12$ components.

Each component is represented as a d-dimensional embedding vector. The embedding matrix which contains all such vectors is denoted as $E \in \mathbb{R}^{d \times |V|}$, where V is the vocabulary of unique lemmas, XPOS, UPOS and dependency edge labels, observed in the training data.

The embedding vectors for the two nodes under consideration are (1) concatenated to form the input to the classifier, (2) projected onto a lower-dimensional space via a linear transformation, (3) squeezed further via another linear transformation followed by applying the Leaky ReLu function (Maas et al., 2013). The last layer of the network consists of one node, followed by the sigmoid function. The decision of whether to insert node n_j to the right or to the left of node n_i is made according to the following rule:

$$decision = \begin{cases} \text{right,} & \text{if } o \geq 0.5, \\ \text{left,} & \text{otherwise.} \end{cases}$$

The neural network components were implemented using PyTorch (Paszke et al., 2017). No pretrained embedding vectors or other external resources were used for the experiments.

4.2 Morphological Component

To create a sentence from an ordered sequence of lemmas, we need to predict the correct morphological form for each of them. This is the purpose of the second component of our system. While we focused mostly on the syntactic realization component, as part of the system development we experimented with the following three different morphological inflection models:

| | | | | | Language | | | | | |
Accuracy (nocase)	ar	cs	en	es	fi	fr	it	nl	pt	ru
LEMMA	13.47	56.43	85.47	71.45	44.43	70.44	67.88	79.35	74.19	50.06
MAJOR	69.15	63.50	86.80	76.13	51.04	74.02	72.48	82.74	75.85	55.64
MORHPMLP	86.63 ± 0.507	94.40 ± 0.052	96.41 ± 0.053	96.72 ± 0.151	78.26 ± 0.217	92.73 ± 0.094	94.09 ± 0.062	91.05 ± 0.110	94.12 ± 0.198	90.43 ± 0.122
MORPHRNNSOFT	88.48 ± 2.409	96.61 ± 0.598	93.57 ± 1.370	97.20 ± 0.801	81.05 ± 7.405	92.30 ± 0.797	92.54 ± 3.721	85.82 ± 1.993	94.27 ± 3.424	93.65 ± 2.980
MORPHRNNHARD	$\mathbf{93.07 \pm 0.515}$	$\mathbf{99.53 \pm 0.031}$	$\mathbf{98.11 \pm 0.054}$	$\mathbf{99.59 \pm 0.027}$	$\mathbf{95.46 \pm 0.923}$	$\mathbf{95.56 \pm 0.066}$	$\mathbf{97.44 \pm 0.240}$	$\mathbf{95.68 \pm 0.115}$	$\mathbf{99.30 \pm 0.035}$	$\mathbf{98.22 \pm 0.056}$
Accuracy (case)										
MORPHMLP	86.63 ± 0.507	87.31 ± 0.083	88.79 ± 0.169	93.52 ± 0.195	71.90 ± 0.286	88.17 ± 0.128	89.54 ± 0.085	85.79 ± 0.236	89.90 ± 0.171	83.32 ± 0.152
MORPHRNNSOFT	88.48 ± 2.409	89.98 ± 0.638	86.32 ± 1.446	94.15 ± 0.823	75.65 ± 6.869	87.90 ± 0.803	88.05 ± 3.524	80.69 ± 1.903	90.06 ± 3.379	87.70 ± 2.763
MORPHRNNHARD	$\mathbf{93.07 \pm 0.515}$	$\mathbf{93.07 \pm 0.047}$	$\mathbf{90.76 \pm 0.186}$	$\mathbf{96.60 \pm 0.037}$	$\mathbf{89.32 \pm 0.861}$	$\mathbf{91.24 \pm 0.099}$	$\mathbf{93.08 \pm 0.296}$	$\mathbf{90.58 \pm 0.219}$	$\mathbf{95.19 \pm 0.119}$	$\mathbf{92.32 \pm 0.079}$

Table 2: Evaluation of the morphological inflection system component on the original UD development set using the percentage of exact string matches as a metric. For the neural architectures, we report both case-sensitive and case-insensitive mean scores and standard deviation (averaged across ten random seed values).

- a simple multi-layer perceptron similar to the one employed for the syntactic component (MORHPMLP)

- an encoder-decoder architecture with an attention mechanism of Bahdanau et al. (2014) (MORHRNNSOFT)

- an encoder-decoder model with a hard monotonic attention (Aharoni and Goldberg, 2017) (MORPHRNNHARD)

OOV lemmas and characters during decoding were copied without any changes.

5 Experimental Setup and Evaluation

Training data was filtered to exclude outliers according to the results of the data analysis (Section 3). The system components were trained separately ten times with different random seeds. In this section, we report mean scores and standard deviation for each model evaluated on the development data and averaged across the random seed values. The evaluation of the proposed approach was done both independently for each of the single components and as a whole in the pipeline mode. All the results are computed on the tokenized data instances.

Morphological component. We start with the evaluation of the morphological inflection generator, and report the exact string match accuracy for each of the tested approaches (Table 2). Two simple baselines were developed for the experiment: given a lemma, LEMMA copies the lemma itself as a prediction of the surface form, MAJOR outputs the most frequent surface form if the lemma is not an OOV item, or the lemma itself, otherwise. Lemma-form frequencies were computed on the training data. For the baselines, we report case-insensitive scores only; the results can be easily extrapolated to the case-sensitive scenario.

As expected, the baselines are outperformed by all data-driven methods examined. Strong performance of the majority baseline for English and Dutch data can be attributed to the simpler morphology of the languages.

The best results are achieved by the model of Aharoni and Goldberg (2017) (MORPHRNNHARD), which outperforms all other methods across all languages. Despite the fact that the approach has a bias towards languages with concatenative morphology (due to the assumption of the monotonic alignment between the input and output character sequences), it also performs well on Arabic. This model was chosen for our further pipeline experiments.

Bad sample complexity of the soft attention model (MORPHRNNSOFT) explains its inferior performance compared to the hard attention model. MORPHRNNSOFT model seems to be highly sensitive to the different values of hyperparameters; its performance has the highest standard deviation among all models, which is most likely due to the same sample complexity issue. Interestingly enough, on English, French, Italian and Dutch data the multi-layer perceptron architecture (MORPHMLP) achieves better results. The latter has a considerably simpler, but less flexible structure, which prohibits the usage of such networks for languages with rich morphology – the number of parameters needed to account for various forms and morphological features grows rapidly until the model can no longer fit into the memory. This also highlights the importance of cross-lingual evaluation of morphological analyzers and generators.

In order to better understand the most common errors made by each of the approaches (excluding the baselines), we examined the predictions of the models on the English development set. We filtered out incorrect predictions of capitalization of

Error types	MorphMlp	MorphRnnSoft	MorphRnnHard
wrong lemma	42	–	–
wrong form	29	8	26
alt. form	29	17	57
non-exist. form	–	29	4
proper noun err.	–	27	–
wrong digit seq.	–	13	–

Table 3: Major error types made by each of the tested morphological component models.

the first letter of the word, because these cases are ignored by the official evaluation protocol. After the filtering, we randomly sampled one hundred erroneous predictions and manually examined them; the results are shown in Table 3.

Unlike character-based models, MorphMlp treats each surface form as an atomic unit and is therefore prone to errors caused by the data sparsity issues, failing to predict correct forms for unseen lemmas or unseen grammar patterns (*wrong lemma* error type). If the model correctly identifies the base form and still makes a mistake, in half of the cases it is an incorrect prediction of verb tenses, singular/plural noun forms or indefinite English articles (*wrong form*). The latter cases are caused by the fact that our model does not use any information about the next token when predicting the form of the current lemma. This limitation is inherent to the pipeline architecture we employed and can be accounted for in a joint morphology/syntax modeling scenario. Finally, there are also cases where a model predicts an alternative surface form which does not match the ground truth, but is grammatically correct (*alt. form*): "not" vs. "n't", "are" vs. "'re", "have" vs. "'ve"). Strictly speaking, the latter cases are not errors, but for simplicity we will treat them as such in this section.

MorphRnnSoft model predicts fewer wrong morphological variants, but suffers from another problem – hallucinating non-existing surface forms: "singed" instead of "sung", "dened" instead of "denied", "siaseme" vs. "siamese". This is not surprising, given the sequential nature of the model; usually this happens in cases with flat probability distributions over a number of possible characters following the already predicted character sequence. A large portion of such errors includes incorrect spellings of proper nouns (*proper noun err*): "Jersualm" vs. "Jerusalem", "Mconal" instead of "Mc-Donal". Finally, one prominent group of errors is that of incorrect digit sequences. MorphMlp does not make these mistakes, because it uses a heuristic:

OOV lemmas are copied verbatim as predictions of the surface forms.

The majority of erroneous cases for MorphRnnHard model constitute the group of alternative forms. Compared to other models, there are considerably fewer cases of predicting non-existent forms ("allergys", "goining"). The *wrong form* error type is mainly represented by incorrect predictions of verb forms: "sing" instead of "sung", "got" instead of "gotten", "are" instead of "'m", etc.

The results of the error analysis suggest that there is still a large room for improvement of the morphological inflection generation component. A principled approach to handling unseen tokens and a way to constrain the predictions to well-formed outputs would be interesting directions to investigate further.

Syntactic component. The syntactic component has been evaluated by computing system-level BLEU, NIST and edit distance scores (Table 4). Following the official evaluation protocol, output texts were normalized prior to computing metrics by lower-casing all tokens.

To the best of our knowledge, surface realization systems have not been evaluated on all the data used in the shared task. A simple baseline (Rand) which outputs a random permutation of the sentence tokens performs poorly across all languages. Compared to it, the 74.88% of the development data sentences ordered correctly by our method seem to indicate a good performance.

To get an idea of where our approach breaks, we sampled a few erroneous predictions and examined them manually. Generally speaking, the syntactic ordering procedure works well on the deeper tree levels, but as we move up, it gets harder to account for the many descendants a node has. An example of this error mode is given in Figure 5.

We tried to improve the prediction capabilities of the system by incorporating feature representations of the leftmost and the rightmost descendant nodes and conditioning the model on the previous pre-

| BLEU | Language | | | | | | | | | |
	ar	cs	en	es	fi	fr	it	nl	pt	ru
RAND	0.013	0.023	0.026	0.016	0.031	0.018	0.022	0.024	0.020	0.024
SYNMLP	0.896 ± 0.003	0.778 ± 0.005	0.889 ± 0.007	0.812 ± 0.005	0.762 ± 0.008	0.889 ± 0.005	0.849 ± 0.006	0.800 ± 0.007	0.901 ± 0.004	0.820 ± 0.005
EDIST										
RAND	0.078	0.115	0.149	0.089	0.139	0.104	0.110	0.126	0.127	0.120
SYNMLP	0.910 ± 0.004	0.833 ± 0.004	0.912 ± 0.006	0.840 ± 0.006	0.827 ± 0.007	0.897 ± 0.005	0.849 ± 0.007	0.844 ± 0.007	0.924 ± 0.005	0.839 ± 0.005
NIST										
RAND	10.40	11.86	9.88	9.78	11.18	9.86	9.40	9.45	9.05	11.35
SYNMLP	14.14 ± 0.011	15.83 ± 0.022	13.97 ± 0.025	14.51 ± 0.030	13.09 ± 0.019	14.48 ± 0.018	12.92 ± 0.016	12.59 ± 0.017	12.87 ± 0.014	15.49 ± 0.025

Table 4: Evaluation of the syntactic ordering component on the original UD development set. We report mean scores and standard deviation for the SYNMLP model; the scores were averaged over ten models trained with different random seeds. RAND is the random baseline. The scores are case-insensitive.

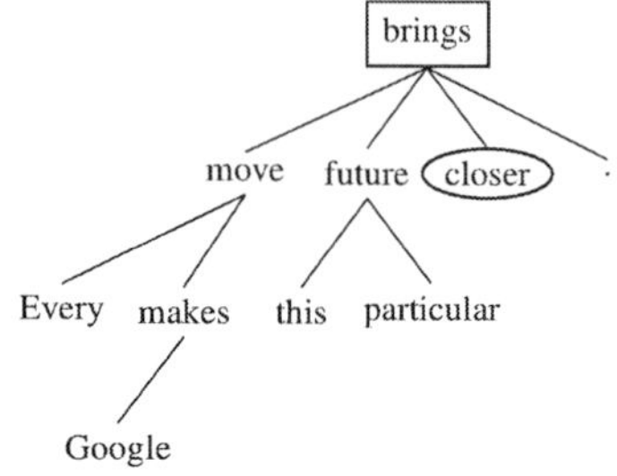

Every move Google makes brings this particular future closer.

Every move Google makes closer brings this particular future.

Figure 5: A common error our syntactic ordering component makes. The node in the rectangle is current head, the node in the oval indicates its child for which the position prediction was incorrect. The upper sentence is the gold ordering, the one below is predicted by our system.

dictions, but this did not yield any improvements. Further investigation with regard to this issue is reserved for future work.

Full pipeline. Table 5 shows the metric evaluation results of the pipeline on the development and test data provided by the organizers (Dev-SR and Test-SR), as well as the development data from the original UD dataset, which was used in our preliminary experiments (Dev-UD).

Given the large gap between the system performance on Dev-SR and Dev-UD, we manually inspected the predictions and observed that the Dev-SR outputs were less grammatical than those made for the Dev-UD data. We investigated the issue and discovered that the morphological component worked as expected, but the syntactic ordering module was flawed. The proposed method's performance varies depending on the children nodes' order returned by the BFS procedure (line 4 of Algorithm 1). Figure 6 shows an example where our

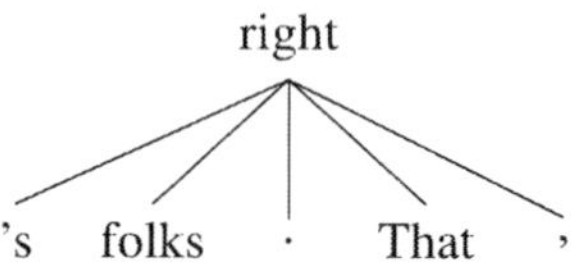

Figure 6: An example sentence which poses a challenge to our system: "That 's right , folks ."

system fails.

It is easier to determine the order of node's children starting with content words and then inserting punctuation signs; if it is the other way round, ordering tokens becomes harder. As mentioned in Section 3, we have used the original UD training and development data which contains token information in the natural order of token occurrence in the sentences. However, in the shared task data the word order information was removed by randomized scrambling of the tokens, which made it harder for the syntactic linearizer to make predictions on Dev-SR and Test-SR. Unfortunately, we did not anticipate that this will have such a great influence on the prediction capabilities of the proposed approach. We plan to investigate ways of improving it in future.

6   Discussion and Future Work

This section summarizes our findings and outlines perspectives for future work. The syntactic ordering component which we propose is capable of performing accurate tree linearization, but its performance varies depending on the order in which nodes are being inserted into the binary tree. Permuting the tokens randomly and training the syntactic component on scrambled token sequences seems to be the easiest way of solving the issue. However, this heuristic method does not guarantee that the model will not encounter an unseen input sequence order, in which case it could fail.

					Language					
BLEU	**ar**	**cs**	**en**	**es**	**fi**	**fr**	**it**	**nl**	**pt**	**ru**
Dev-UD	0.757	0.782	0.862	0.816	0.701	0.800	0.805	0.733	0.888	0.796
Dev-SR	0.148	0.250	0.291	0.332	0.230	0.244	0.225	0.221	0.261	0.34
Test-SR	0.162	0.251	0.296	0.322	0.233	0.205	0.236	0.227	0.246	0.343
EDIST										
Dev-UD	0.854	0.840	0.909	0.851	0.808	0.868	0.837	0.824	0.922	0.835
Dev-SR	0.192	0.239	0.359	0.274	0.294	0.270	0.258	0.252	0.343	0.318
Test-SR	0.444	0.357	0.659	0.370	0.412	0.286	0.407	0.482	0.514	0.346
NIST										
Dev-UD	12.91	15.79	13.64	14.47	12.44	13.63	12.48	11.85	12.78	15.5
Dev-SR	6.64	10.61	9.40	10.23	9.35	8.68	7.73	8.61	7.76	12.94
Test-SR	6.94	10.74	9.58	10.21	9.36	7.21	7.60	8.64	7.54	13.06

Table 5: Final metric evaluation results of the system pipeline. Dev-UD denotes the development set of the original UD dataset. Dev-SR and Test-SR is the data provided by the organizers (with scrambled lemmas).

A more principled approach would be to define an adaptive model which encodes some notion of processing preference: given a set of tokens, the system should first make predictions it is most confident about, similar to easy-first dependency parsing algorithm (Goldberg and Elhadad, 2010) or imitation learning methods (Lampouras and Vlachos, 2016).

Another limitation of the proposed method is its inability to handle non-projective dependencies. This is a simplification decision we made when designing the algorithm: at each point we assume that the perfect token order can be retrieved by recursively ordering head-children subtrees, which excludes long-range crossing dependencies from consideration. By doing so we aggressively prune the search space and simplify the inference procedure, but also rule out a smaller class of more complex constructions. This might not be a problem for the English UD data, which has a small number of non-projective dependencies. However, according to the empirical study of Nivre (2006), almost 25% of the sentences in the Prague Dependency Treebank of Czech (Böhmová, Alena and Hajič, Jan and Hajičová, Eva and Hladká, Barbora, 2003), and more than 15% in the Danish Dependency Treebank (Kromann, 2003) contain non-projective dependencies. This implies that for multi-lingual surface realization such an assumption could be too strong.

Finally, another simplification which could be addressed is the decomposition of the prediction process into two separate stages of syntactic ordering and word inflection. The benefits of joint morphological inflection and syntactic ordering have been previously explored, but we found no easy way of doing so for the proposed approach. Nevertheless, it seems like a promising direction to pursue, and we plan to investigate it further.

7 Conclusion

In this paper, we have presented the results of our participation in the Surface Realization Shared Task 2018. We developed a promising method of syntactic ordering; evaluation results on the development data indicate that once the problem of order-sensitivity is solved, it can be successfully applied as a component in the syntactic realization pipeline.

Acknowledgments

This work was supported by the German Research Foundation (DFG) under grant No.GU 798/17-1 and the DFG-funded research training group "Adaptive Preparation of Information form Heterogeneous Sources" (AIPHES, GRK 1994/1). The first author of the paper is supported by the FAZIT Foundation scholarship. We thank Claire Gardent for the insightful comments and our colleagues Michael Bugert, Tobias Falke, Jan-Christoph Klie, Ji-Ung Lee and Nils Reimers who provided suggestions that greatly assisted our research. Calculations for this research were conducted on the Lichtenberg high performance computer of TU Darmstadt.

References

Roee Aharoni and Yoav Goldberg. 2017. Morphological Inflection Generation with Hard Monotonic Attention. In *Proceedings of the 55th Annual Meeting of the Association for Computational Linguistics (Volume 1: Long Papers)*, pages 2004–2015, Vancouver, Canada. Association for Computational Linguistics.

Malin Ahlberg, Markus Forsberg, and Mans Hulden. 2015. Paradigm Classification in Supervised Learning of Morphology. In *Proceedings of the 2015 Conference of the North American Chapter of the Association for Computational Linguistics: Human Language Technologies*, pages 1024–1029, Denver, Colorado. Association for Computational Linguistics.

Dzmitry Bahdanau, Kyunghyun Cho, and Yoshua Bengio. 2014. Neural Machine Translation by Jointly Learning to Align and Translate. *CoRR*, abs/1409.0473.

Srinivas Bangalore and Owen Rambow. 2000. Exploiting a Probabilistic Hierarchical Model for Generation. In *Proceedings of the 18th Conference on Computational Linguistics: Volume 1*, pages 42–48, Saarbrücken, Germany. Association for Computational Linguistics.

Anja Belz, Mike White, Dominic Espinosa, Eric Kow, Deirdre Hogan, and Amanda Stent. 2011. The First Surface Realisation Shared Task: Overview and Evaluation Results. In *Proceedings of the Generation Challenges Session at the 13th European Workshop on Natural Language Generation*, pages 217–226, Nancy, France. Association for Computational Linguistics.

Böhmová, Alena and Hajič, Jan and Hajičová, Eva and Hladká, Barbora. 2003. *The Prague Dependency Treebank: a Three-level Annotation Scenario*, chapter 7. Kluwer Academic Publishers.

Bernd Bohnet, Leo Wanner, Simon Mille, and Alicia Burga. 2010. Broad Coverage Multilingual Deep Sentence Generation with a Stochastic Multi-level Realizer. In *Proceedings of the 23rd International Conference on Computational Linguistics*, pages 98–106, Beijing, China. Association for Computational Linguistics.

John Carroll, Ann Copestake, Dan Flickinger, and Victor Poznanski. 1999. An Efficient Chart Generator for (Semi-)Lexicalist Grammars. In *Proceedings of the 7th European Workshop on Natural Language Generation*, pages 86–95, Toulouse, France.

Kyunghyun Cho, Bart van Merrienboer, Caglar Gulcehre, Dzmitry Bahdanau, Fethi Bougares, Holger Schwenk, and Yoshua Bengio. 2014. Learning Phrase Representations Using RNN Encoder-decoder for Statistical Machine Translation. In *Proceedings of the 2014 Conference on Empirical Methods in Natural Language Processing (EMNLP)*, pages 1724–1734, Doha, Qatar. Association for Computational Linguistics.

George Doddington. 2002. Automatic Evaluation of Machine Translation Quality Using N-gram Co-occurrence Statistics. In *Proceedings of the Second International Conference on Human Language Technology Research*, pages 138–145, San Francisco, CA, USA. Morgan Kaufmann Publishers Inc.

Markus Dreyer and Jason Eisner. 2011. Discovering Morphological Paradigms from Plain Text Using a Dirichlet Process Mixture Model. In *Proceedings of the 2011 Conference on Empirical Methods in Natural Language Processing*, pages 616–627, Edinburgh, Scotland, UK. Association for Computational Linguistics.

Greg Durrett and John DeNero. 2013. Supervised Learning of Complete Morphological Paradigms. In *Proceedings of the 2013 Conference of the North American Chapter of the Association for Computational Linguistics: Human Language Technologies*, pages 1185–1195, Atlanta, Georgia. Association for Computational Linguistics.

Michael Elhadad and Jacques Robin. 1992. Controlling Content Realization with Functional Unification Grammars. In *Proceedings of the 6th International Workshop on Natural Language Generation: Aspects of Automated Natural Language Generation*, pages 89–104, London, UK, UK. Springer-Verlag.

Manaal Faruqui, Yulia Tsvetkov, Graham Neubig, and Chris Dyer. 2016. Morphological Inflection Generation Using Character Sequence to Sequence Learning. In *Proceedings of the 2016 Conference of the North American Chapter of the Association for Computational Linguistics: Human Language Technologies*, pages 634–643, San Diego, California. Association for Computational Linguistics.

Yoav Goldberg and Michael Elhadad. 2010. An Efficient Algorithm for Easy-first Non-directional Dependency Parsing. In *Human Language Technologies: The 2010 Annual Conference of the North American Chapter of the Association for Computational Linguistics*, pages 742–750, Los Angeles, California. Association for Computational Linguistics.

Yuqing Guo, Josef van Genabith, and Haifeng Wang. 2008. Dependency-based N-gram Models for General Purpose Sentence Realisation. In *Proceedings of the 22nd International Conference on Computational Linguistics (COLING 2008)*, pages 297–304, Manchester, UK. COLING 2008 Organizing Committee.

Wei He, Haifeng Wang, Yuqing Guo, and Ting Liu. 2009. Dependency Based Chinese Sentence Realization. In *Proceedings of the Joint Conference of the 47th Annual Meeting of the ACL and the 4th International Joint Conference on Natural Language Processing of the AFNLP: Volume 2 - Volume 2*, ACL '09, pages 809–816, Suntec, Singapore. Association for Computational Linguistics.

Ronald M. Kaplan and Martin Kay. 1994. Regular Models of Phonological Rule Systems. *Computational Linguistics*, 20(3):331–378.

Kimmo Koskenniemi. 1983. Two-level Morphology: a General Computational Model for Word-form Recognition and Production. *Publications*, 11:1–160.

Matthias Trautner Kromann. 2003. The Danish Dependency Treebank and the DTAG Treebank Tool. In *Proceedings of the 2nd Workshop on Treebanks and Linguistic Theories*, pages 217–220.

Gerasimos Lampouras and Andreas Vlachos. 2016. Imitation Learning for Language Generation from Unaligned Data. In *Proceedings of COLING 2016, the 26th International Conference on Computational Linguistics: Technical Papers*, pages 1101–1112, Osaka, Japan. The COLING 2016 Organizing Committee.

Irene Langkilde-Geary. 2002. An Empirical Verification of Coverage and Correctness for a General-purpose Sentence Generator. In *Proceedings of the 2nd International Natural Language Generation Conference*, pages 17–24, Harriman, New York, USA.

Yijia Liu, Yue Zhang, Wanxiang Che, and Bing Qin. 2015. Transition-based Syntactic Linearization. In *Proceedings of the 2015 Conference of the North American Chapter of the Association for Computational Linguistics: Human Language Technologies*, pages 113–122, Denver, Colorado. Association for Computational Linguistics.

Andrew L. Maas, Awni Y. Hannun, and Andrew Y. Ng. 2013. Rectifier Nonlinearities Improve Neural Network Acoustic Models. In *ICML Workshop on Deep Learning for Audio, Speech and Language Processing*, Atlanta, USA.

Simon Mille, Anja Belz, Bernd Bohnet, Yvette Graham, Emily Pitler, and Leo Wanner. 2018. The First Multilingual Surface Realisation Shared Task (SR'18): Overview and Evaluation Results. In *Proceedings of the 1st Workshop on Multilingual Surface Realisation (MSR), 56th Annual Meeting of the Association for Computational Linguistics (ACL)*, pages 1–10, Melbourne, Australia.

Joakim Nivre. 2006. Constraints on Non-Projective Dependency Parsing. In *Proceedings of the 11th Conference of the European Chapter of the Association for Computational Linguistics*, pages 73–80, Trento, Italy. Association for Computational Linguistics.

Kishore Papineni, Salim Roukos, Todd Ward, and Wei-Jing Zhu. 2002. BLEU: a Method for Automatic Evaluation of Machine Translation. In *Proceedings of 40th Annual Meeting of the Association for Computational Linguistics*, pages 311–318, Philadelphia, Pennsylvania, USA. Association for Computational Linguistics.

Adam Paszke, Sam Gross, Soumith Chintala, Gregory Chanan, Edward Yang, Zachary DeVito, Zeming Lin, Alban Desmaison, Luca Antiga, and Adam Lerer. 2017. Automatic Differentiation in PyTorch. In *NIPS 2017 Workshop Autodiff*, Long Beach, California, USA.

Ratish Puduppully, Yue Zhang, and Manish Shrivastava. 2016. Transition-based Syntactic Linearization with Lookahead Features. In *Proceedings of the 2016 Conference of the North American Chapter of the Association for Computational Linguistics: Human Language Technologies*, pages 488–493, San Diego, California. Association for Computational Linguistics.

Ilya Sutskever, Oriol Vinyals, and Quoc V Le. 2014. Sequence to Sequence Learning with Neural Networks. In Z. Ghahramani, M. Welling, C. Cortes, N. D. Lawrence, and K. Q. Weinberger, editors, *Advances in Neural Information Processing Systems 27*, pages 3104–3112. Curran Associates, Inc.

Ramakrishna Vedantam, C. Lawrence Zitnick, and Devi Parikh. 2015. CIDEr: Consensus-based Image Description Evaluation. In *2015 IEEE Conference on Computer Vision and Pattern Recognition (CVPR)*, pages 4566–4575, Boston, MA, USA. IEEE Computer Society.

Michael White, Rajakrishnan Rajkumar, and Scott Martin. 2007. Towards Broad Coverage Surface Realization with CCG. In *Proceedings of the 2007 Workshop on Using Corpora for NLG: Language Generation and Machine Translation (UCNLG+MT)*, pages 22–30, Copenhagen, Danmark.

Richard Wicentowski. 2004. Multilingual Noise-robust Supervised Morphological Analysis Using the Wordframe Model. In *Proceedings of the 7th Meeting of the ACL Special Interest Group in Computational Phonology: Current Themes in Computational Phonology and Morphology*, SIGMorPhon '04, pages 70–77, Barcelona, Spain. Association for Computational Linguistics.

David Yarowsky and Richard Wicentowski. 2000. Minimally Supervised Morphological Analysis by Multimodal Alignment. In *Proceedings of the 38th Annual Meeting on Association for Computational Linguistics*, ACL '00, pages 207–216, Hong Kong. Association for Computational Linguistics.

Yue Zhang and Stephen Clark. 2011. Syntactic Processing Using the Generalized Perceptron and Beam Search. *Computational Linguistics*, 37(1):105–151.

A Supplementary Material

A.1 Data Analysis Results

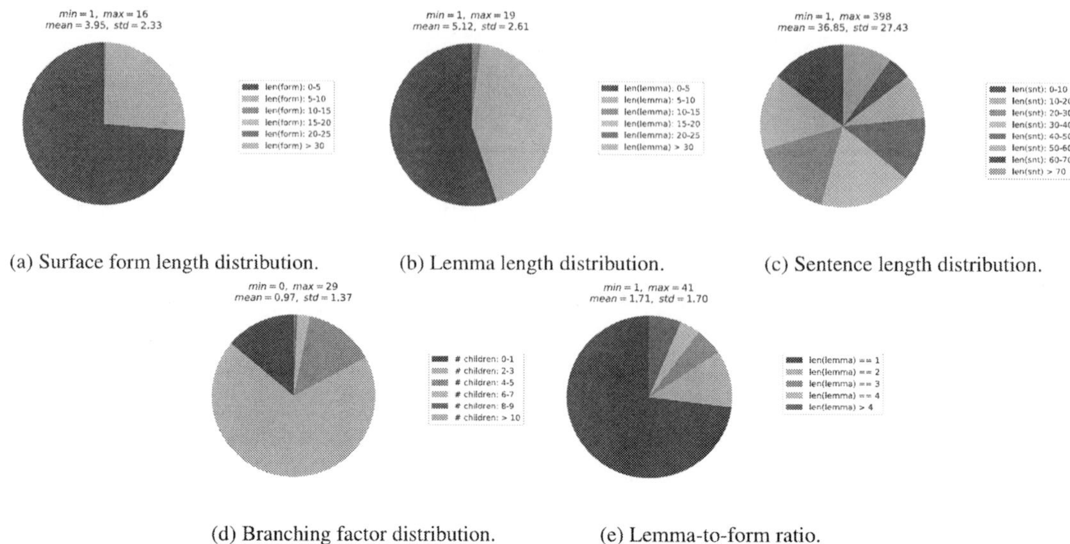

(a) Surface form length distribution.

(b) Lemma length distribution.

(c) Sentence length distribution.

(d) Branching factor distribution.

(e) Lemma-to-form ratio.

Figure 7: Data statistics computed for the Arabic data.

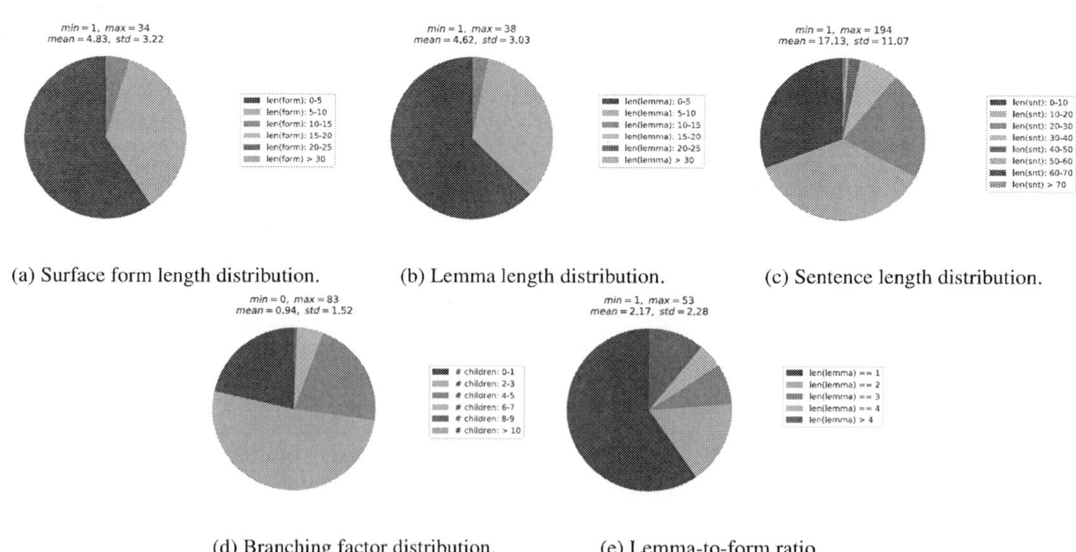

(a) Surface form length distribution.

(b) Lemma length distribution.

(c) Sentence length distribution.

(d) Branching factor distribution.

(e) Lemma-to-form ratio.

Figure 8: Data statistics computed for the Czech data.

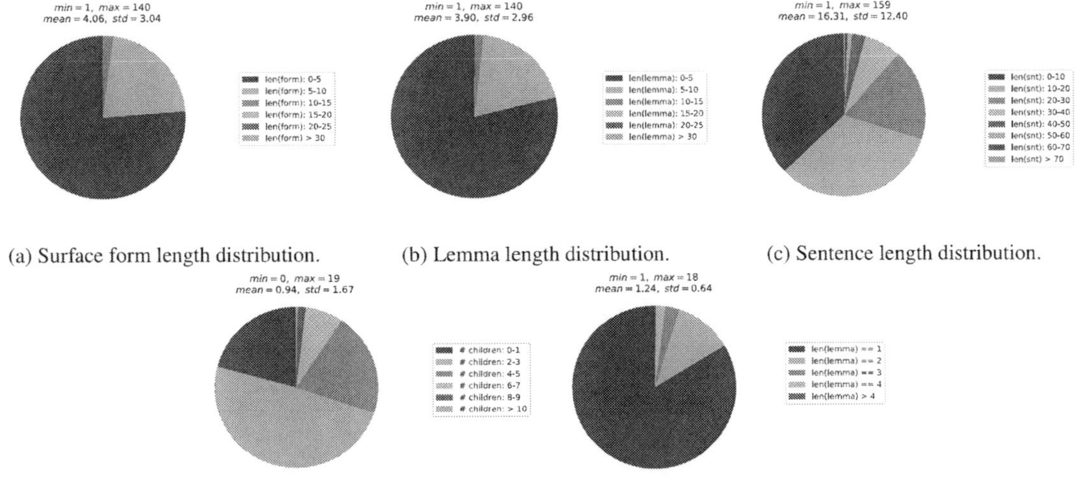

(a) Surface form length distribution.　(b) Lemma length distribution.　(c) Sentence length distribution.

(d) Branching factor distribution.　(e) Lemma-to-form ratio.

Figure 9: Data statistics computed for the English data.

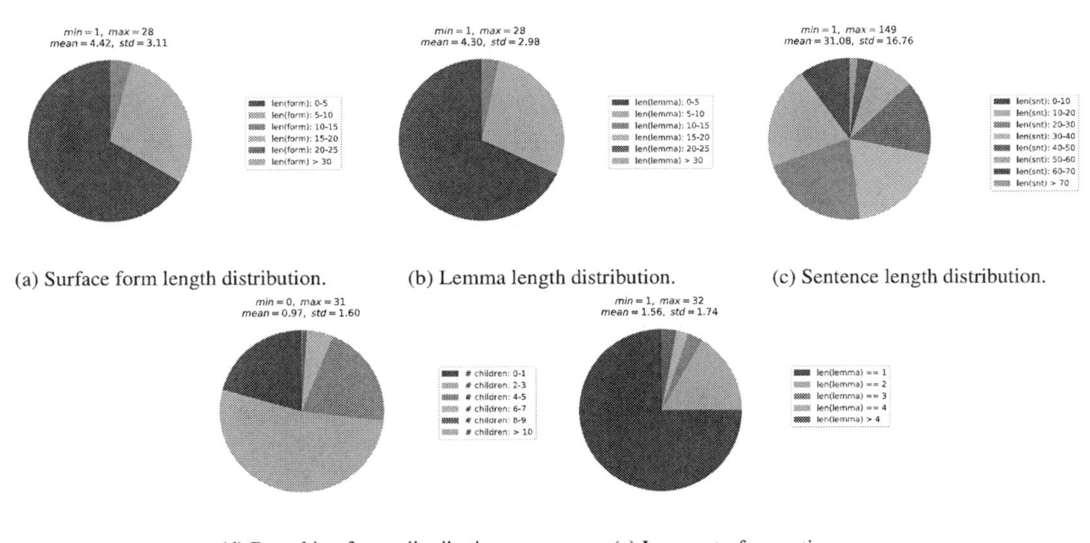

(a) Surface form length distribution.　(b) Lemma length distribution.　(c) Sentence length distribution.

(d) Branching factor distribution.　(e) Lemma-to-form ratio.

Figure 10: Data statistics computed for the Spanish data.

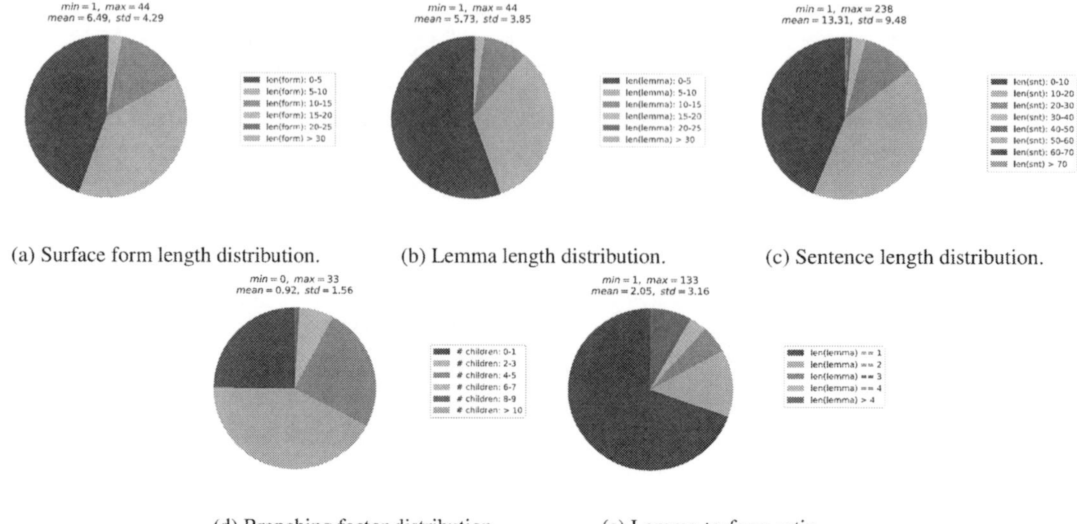

(a) Surface form length distribution. (b) Lemma length distribution. (c) Sentence length distribution.

(d) Branching factor distribution. (e) Lemma-to-form ratio.

Figure 11: Data statistics computed for the Finnish data.

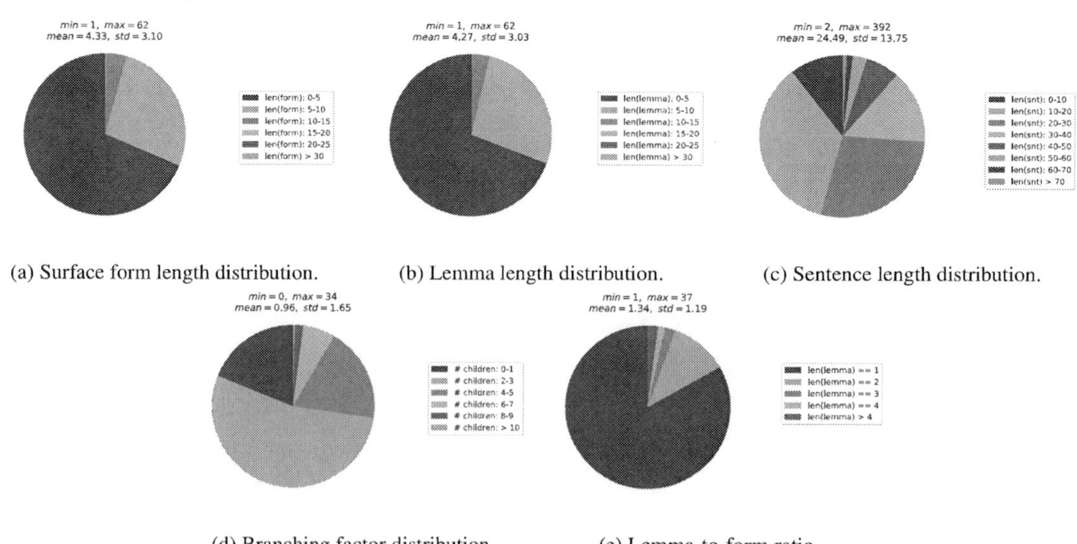

(a) Surface form length distribution. (b) Lemma length distribution. (c) Sentence length distribution.

(d) Branching factor distribution. (e) Lemma-to-form ratio.

Figure 12: Data statistics computed for the French data.

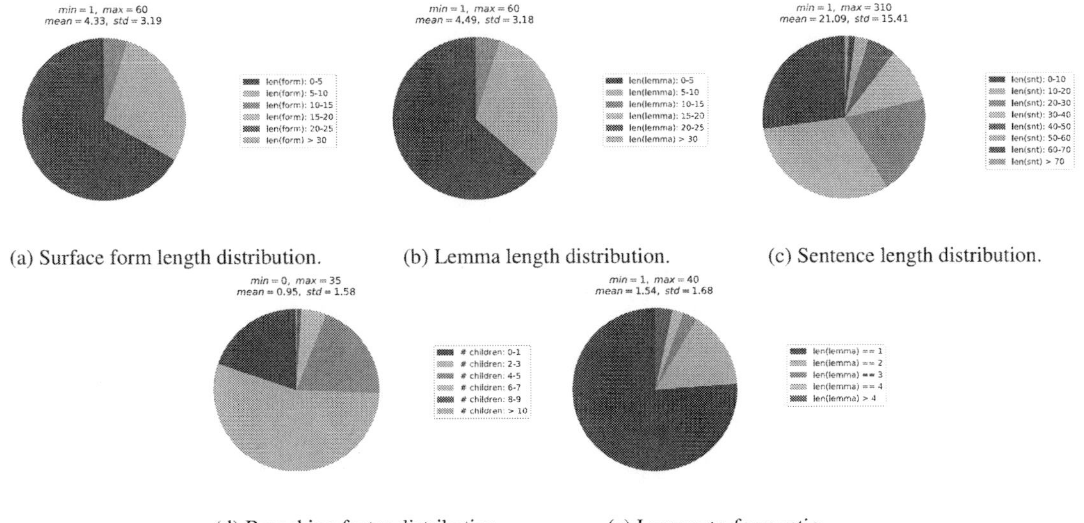

(a) Surface form length distribution.　　(b) Lemma length distribution.　　(c) Sentence length distribution.

(d) Branching factor distribution.　　(e) Lemma-to-form ratio.

Figure 13: Data statistics computed for the Italian data.

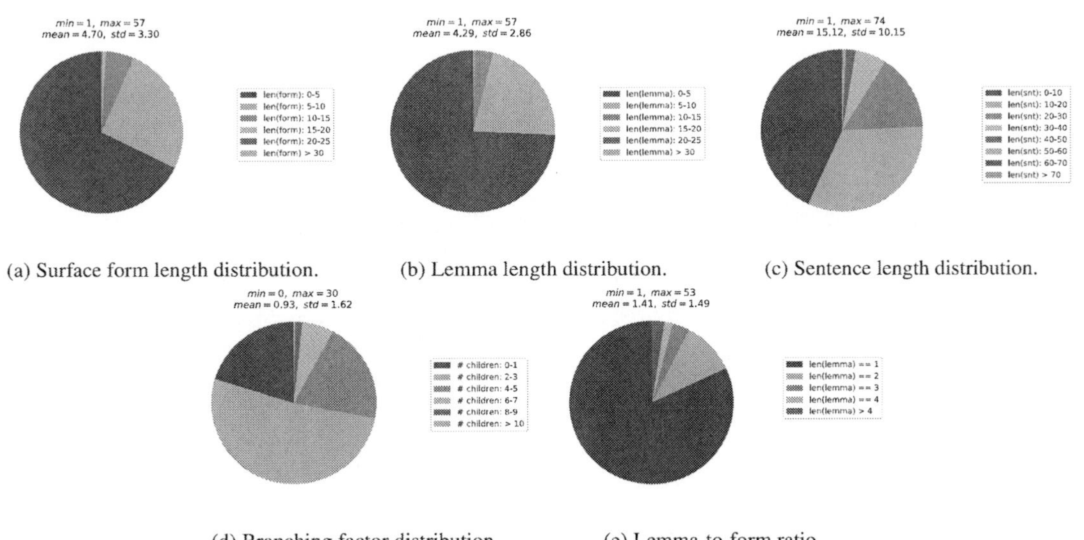

(a) Surface form length distribution.　　(b) Lemma length distribution.　　(c) Sentence length distribution.

(d) Branching factor distribution.　　(e) Lemma-to-form ratio.

Figure 14: Data statistics computed for the Dutch data.

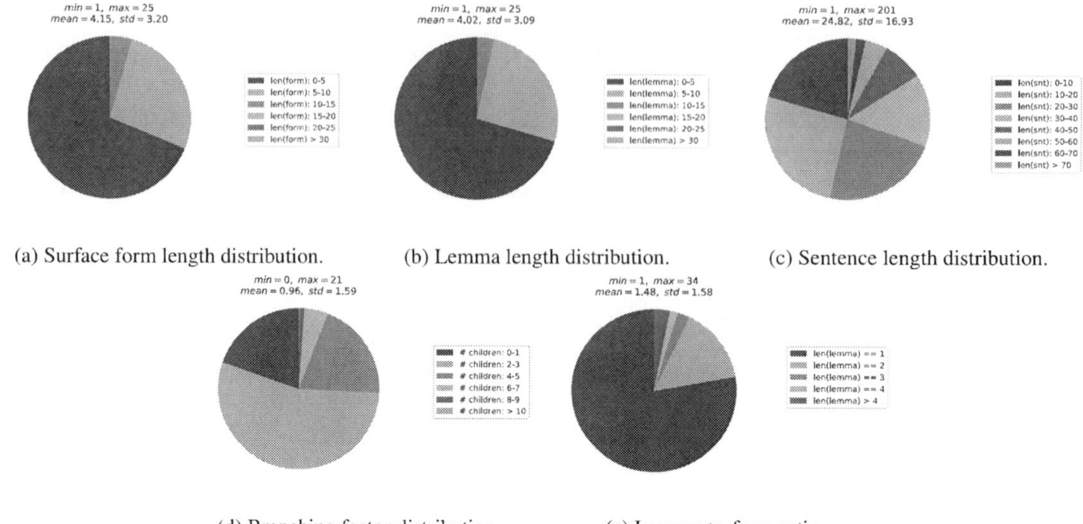

(a) Surface form length distribution.   (b) Lemma length distribution.   (c) Sentence length distribution.

(d) Branching factor distribution.   (e) Lemma-to-form ratio.

Figure 15: Data statistics computed for the Portuguese data.

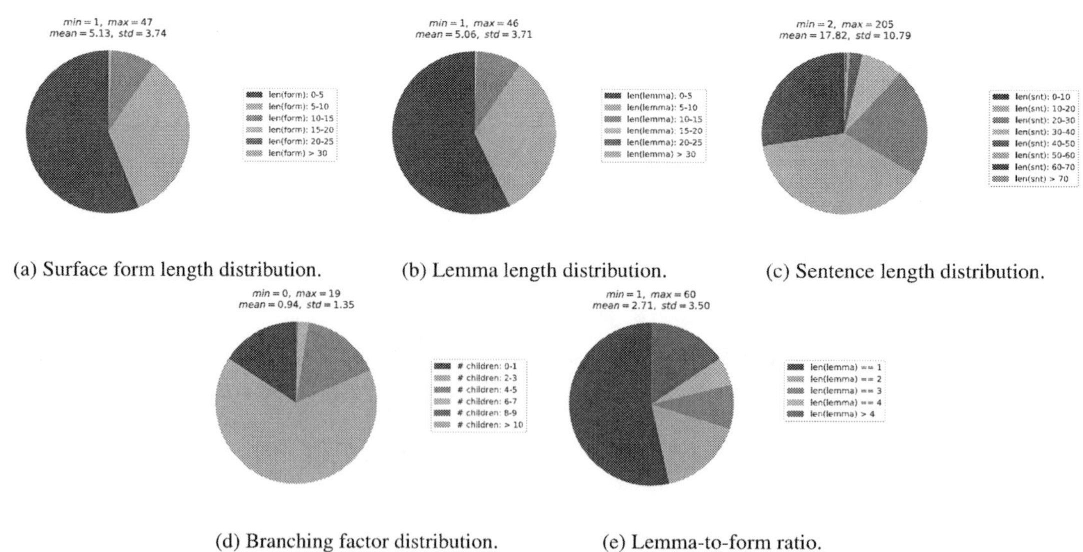

(a) Surface form length distribution.   (b) Lemma length distribution.   (c) Sentence length distribution.

(d) Branching factor distribution.   (e) Lemma-to-form ratio.

Figure 16: Data statistics computed for the Russian data.

IIT (BHU) Varanasi at MSR-SRST 2018: A Language Model Based Approach for Natural Language Generation

Avi Chawla, Ayush Sharma, Shreyansh Singh and A.K. Singh

Indian Institute of Technology (BHU), Varanasi, India
{avi.chawla.cse16,ayush.sharma.cse16}@iitbhu.ac.in
{shreyansh.singh.cse16,aksingh.cse}@iitbhu.ac.in

Abstract

This paper describes our submission system for the Shallow Track of Surface Realization Shared Task 2018 (SRST'18). The task was to convert genuine UD structures, from which word order information had been removed and the tokens had been lemmatized, into their correct sentential form. We divide the problem statement into two parts, word reinflection and correct word order prediction. For the first sub-problem, we use a Long Short Term Memory based Encoder-Decoder approach. For the second sub-problem, we present a Language Model (LM) based approach. We apply two different sub-approaches in the LM Based approach and the combined result of these two approaches is considered as the final output of the system.

1 Introduction

SRST'18 (Mille et al., 2018), organized under ACL 2018, Melbourne, Australia aims to re-obtain the word order information which has been removed from the UD Structures (Nivre et al., 2016). Universal Dependency (UD) structure is a tree representation of the dependency relations between words in a sentence of any language. Made using the UD framework, the structure of the tree is determined by the relation between a word and its dependents. Each node of this tree holds the Part of Speech (PoS) tag and morphological information as found in the original annotations of the word corresponding to that node.
The morphological information of a word includes the information gained from the formation of the word and its relationship with other words. Morphological information includes gender, animacy, number, mood, tense etc.
In this problem, we are given

1. Unordered dependency trees with lemmatized nodes.

2. The nodes hold PoS tags and morphological information as found in the original annotations.

3. The corresponding ordered sentences.

Our system may find its use in various NLP applications like Natural Language Generation (NLG) (Reiter and Dale, 1997). NLG is a major and relatively unexplored sub-field of NLP. Our system can be used in tasks like Question Answering, where you have the knowledge base with you which may not necessarily be holding the correct word order information but must be holding the dependencies between the words. This is where NLG is useful, where you take all the dependencies available with you and try to generate language from it which can be understood and interpreted easily by the person or user. This system also finds its application in other important tasks like abstractive text summarization (Barzilay and McKeown, 2005) and image caption generation (Xu et al., 2015), since having the correct word order is a must for any text.
Our system makes use of a Long Short Term Memory (LSTM) (Hochreiter and Schmidhuber, 1997) based Encoder-Decoder (Sudhakar and Singh, 2017) approach to tackle the subproblem-1 of this track, i.e word re-inflection and then we make use of a probabilistic and statistical Language Model to determine the correct word order from the unordered sentences. Statistical Language Modeling, or Language Modeling or LM in short, is a technique which uses probabilistic models that are able to predict the next word in the sequence given the words that precede it. This is

Proceedings of the First Workshop on Multilingual Surface Realisation, pages 29–34
Melbourne, Australia, July 19, 2018. ©2018 Association for Computational Linguistics

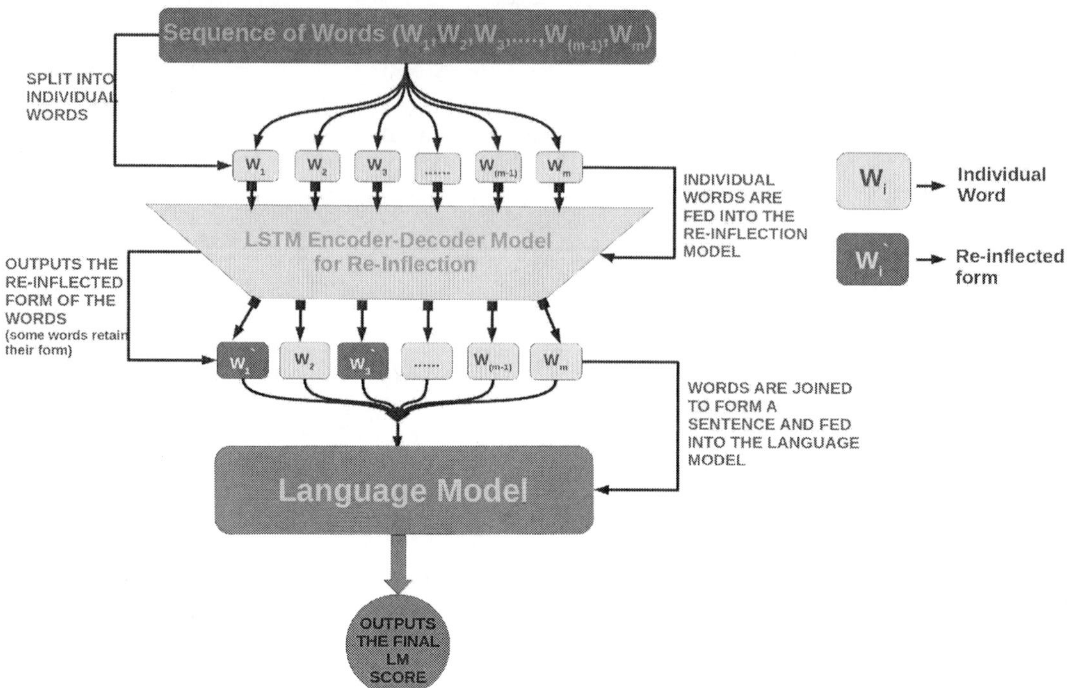

Figure 1: Architecture of the Proposed Model - Word sequence $(w_1, w_2, w_3, ...,w_n)$ is reinfected into $(w'_1, w_2, w'_3, ..., w_m)$, where w'_i are the changed words due to reinfection. Final output gives the LM Score for the sequence of reinflected words. Model is run on different possible combinations and the sequence with best LM Score is chosen.

done by assigning a probability to the whole sequence.

The shared task organizers provided the training and a small development dataset for building our systems. A period of about 3 weeks was given for submitting our predictions on the test set.

The rest of the paper is structured as follows. Section 2 discusses, in brief, the dataset for the task. Section 3 explains our proposed approach in detail. We discuss what models we have used to re-inflect the words and generate ordered sentences from the jumbled sentences. Section 4 explains how the system is evaluated and Section 5 states the results we have obtained. We have also included an analysis of our system in Section 6. We conclude our paper and discuss its future prospects in Section 7.

2   Data

We used the dataset provided by the shared task organizers for training our system. No other external dataset was used in training. The dataset of the shared task is comprised of two sets of files, a .conll file containing the UD structures of sentences, and a text file containing the ordered sentences along with their sentence ids. We have worked only on the English language dataset. There are around 12000 sentences in the training file and approximately 3000 sentences in the development file. The complete details of the dataset can be found here[1].

3   Proposed System

In the Shallow Track of the shared task, we had two subproblems to deal with. First one was the re-inflection problem and the second one involved

___
[1]`http://taln.upf.edu/pages/msr2018-ws/SRST.html#data`

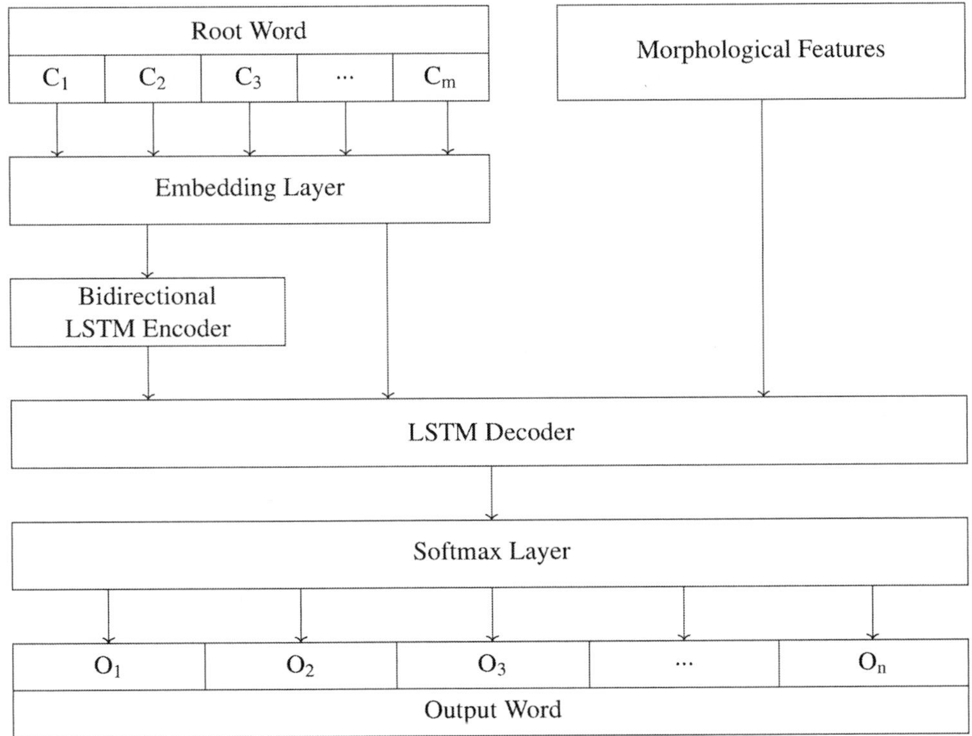

Figure 2: Architecture of the Word Re-inflection model - C_1, .., C_m represent characters of the root word while O_1, ..,O_n represent characters of the output word.

the task of re-obtaining the correct word order from the unordered UD structure. We shall refer to these problems as Subproblem-1 and Subproblem-2 subsequently in this paper. Subproblem-1 is the word re-inflection problem and Subproblem-2 is the word ordering problem.

The complete architecture of the proposed model is shown in Figure 1.

3.1 Sub Problem-1: Word Re-inflection

In the given UD structure, the words are given in lemmatized form. Before proceeding to determine the correct order of words, these lemmatized words must be re-inflected to convert them into their correct form. For the task of re-inflection, we implemented an LSTM based encoder-decoder model. The morphological information is given in CoNLL format. Since majority of the past work in reinfection uses the UniMorph annotation format of the morphological features, we first converted our morphological features from CoNLL to an approximation of the UniMorph format by modeling a manual mapping between the two tagsets. Eg. For the word "preacher", the CoNLL

annotation format is Noun & Number=Sing. We convert this to N;SING. This can be treated as an approximation of the UniMorph annotation format, which is sufficient for us.

This approach is based on a submission in the CoNLL-SIGMORPHON-2017 Shared Task (Sudhakar and Singh, 2017). The model takes into account the fact that the root word (lemmatized form) and the target word (re-inflected form) are similar except for the parts that have been changed due to re-inflection. The model outputs the target word character by character, thus handling both the cases when there are prefix or suffix changes (*play* to *playing*) or changes occurring in the middle of the word (*man* to *men*).

The root word is represented using character indices, while the associated morphological features are represented in the form of a binary vector. A root word embedding for each word is formed by making a 64 dimensional character embedding of each character. This embedding is fed into a bidirectional LSTM encoder. The output of this encoder, along with the root word embedding and the binary vector representing the morphological features, acts as input to the LSTM decoder. A softmax layer is then used to predict the character at each position of the output word. To maintain a common length for all words, a padding of 0 is used. The architecture of this model is shown in Figure 2.

3.2 Sub Problem-2: Word-Ordering

We have used a probabilistic and statistical Language Model to tackle this subproblem. After re-inflecting the words in the UD-Structures, the next step is to obtain the correct word-order of each sentence. For this, we make use of the SRILM Toolkit (Stolcke, 2002).

Before predicting the correct word-order, we follow the following steps to train the Language Model:

1. We generate a vocabulary file from the corpus of ordered sentences. The vocab file is the list of all unique words occurring in the corpus, with each word in a different line.

2. After we have the vocab file with us, we make use of this and the ordered sentence data to generate a .lm file using the SRILM toolkit. This file contains the probability scores of the associated n-grams (till trigrams) present in the corpus.

After calculating these probabilities, we move on to solve the prime objective of this subproblem, which is to find the correct word order of the unordered sentences.

For this, we have used two methods. Selecting which method to use depends on the sentence length.

- Method 1: 4-gram LM Based Approach

- Method 2: Variable n-gram LM Based Approach

Method 1 is used in cases where the sentence length is more than 23 (23 being a hyperparameter in this case) and Method 2 is used for sentences having their length less than or equal to 23. Note that we have predicted the sentences without any punctuations in it. All the punctuations appearing in a sentence were removed. However, a full stop was added at the end of each predicted sentence.

We thoroughly describe the two methods below.

3.2.1 Method 1: 4-gram LM Based Approach

This method is used to find the correct sentential form of those sentences which have length greater than 23. We define the Language Model score (LM score) of a string to be the probability measure of that string being drawn from some vocabulary. If the vocabulary is made using linguistically correct sentences, then a higher Language Model score indicates higher probability of a sentence being linguistically correct. An ideal approach would be to calculate the LM score of all possible permutations of all the words in a sentence and select the permutation with the highest LM score. Since this is computationally very expensive (specially for large sentences), hence we check for permutations of at most 4 words only. If the sentence length is less than or equal to 4, we select the permutation with the highest LM score. For length greater than 3, we calculate the LM score of all the possible 4-grams for the given sentence. Then, we select the one which gives the highest LM score and choose this as the start of the sentence sequence. For determining rest of the sequence, we follow the following steps:

1. Maintain a list of remaining words (LRW). This list consists of all the words in the sentence, except the 4 words which have been selected as the start of the sentence sequence.

2. Repeat the following until no word is left in LRW:

   - For each word left in LRW, check which word, on addition to the predicted sequence gives the maximum Language Model Score. Let this word be w.
   - Add w to the predicted sequence and remove it from LRW.

By following the above mentioned steps, we get the final sequence of words as predicted by Method-1 of our LM approach.

3.2.2 Variable N-gram LM Based Approach

This method was used to find the correct sentential form of those sentences having length less than or equal to 23. In this method, instead of only looking for the best 4-gram, we look for various bigrams and trigrams as well. For example, for a sentence of length 6, we break the sentence into (3-gram, 2-gram, 1-gram), (2-gram, 2-gram, 2-gram) and (3-gram, 3-gram). Similarly, we have manually broken each sentence length into different combination of unigrams, bigrams and trigrams. We calculate the LM score of different relative arrangements of these n-grams. Out of all the possible relative arrangements, the one which gives the maximum LM Score is chosen as the prediction of our model for that jumbled sentence. The idea behind choosing different combinations of n-grams is that a sentence is generally divided into different chunks and if we are able to identify the chunks in which the words of a sentence appear, we can then use a language model to find which possible sequence would have been the best out of all the different possible relative arrangements of these chunks of words.

4 Evaluation

Cross Validation (CV): We trained our model on the training data and did predictions on the development data, both of which were provided by the shared task organizers. These predictions were considered as the CV Score of our model. The metrics that were used to evaluate the model were BLEU (Papineni et al., 2002), NE DIST and NIST (Doddington, 2002). Evaluation script for the same was also provided by the organizers.

Test: Once we were done with the optimal tuning of our model using the CV score, we used our model to generate ordered sentences on the test data. We trained on the full training data for the re-inflection task and combined the training and development data to generate the language model (.lm) file for the word-ordering task.

5 Results

We worked on Track 1 (Shallow track) of the shared task for the English language. The performances of our system, the system which scored the highest for English and the system which scored the highest when averaged over the scores of all the languages is given in the table below. Evaluation is done across various metrics provided by the shared task organizers. Note that all the scores given below are for English language only.

	BLEU Score	NE DIST	NIST
IIT (BHU) Varanasi	8.04	47.63	7.71
Highest for English	69.14	80.42	12.02
Highest Average	55.29	65.9	9.58

Table 1: Scores for English on test data.

For word reinflection, the LSTM based encoder-decoder model correctly predicted the re-inflected forms of 95.8% words when trained on the training dataset and tested on the development dataset.

6 Analysis

Our model for the word reinflection sub-problem produces good results. But, the results for the word reordering sub-problem are not very good. Total 8 teams submitted their systems in the shared task, and our system was ranked the last for English by each of the three metrics given in the Results section. Some of the reasons for this are

- The sentences submitted as output did not have punctuations except a full stop at the end. Because of this, our sentences lacked punctuations occurring inside a sentence. Also, it is not necessary that a sentence ends with a full stop only.

- Enumerating over permutations for the word reordering sub-problem was computationally expensive for sentences of length greater than 23. So, we had to use the 4-gram approach for such sentences, which does not perform that well as the variable n-gram approach. Since there were many sentences having length greater than 23 in the test set, the overall results got adversely affected. For example, *"It looks pretty cool on the other hand."* is a prediction by our model, which is a decent sentence. However, the prediction *"There have been the us soldiers with have to either even long since by arab fundamentalists local sunni radicals become remain or or relations sunnis committed nationalism roiled falluja tense."*, which is 30 words long, does not appear to be a meaningful English sentence.

- There is another important point worth noticing with respect to the evaluation metrics. For a given set of words, there may be more than one linguistically correct word order. For example, both the sentences *"The boy reads a book."* and *"The book a boy reads."* are made up of the same set of words and both are linguistically correct as well. So, the algorithms used for evaluation of results may not give the highest possible score to a sentence even if it is linguistically correct.

7 Conclusion and Future Work

In this paper, we described a system which treats reinflection and word reordering as two independent sub-problems. We have used an LSTM based approach to solve the problem of re-inflection. The LSTM model works on character embeddings and predicts the re-inflected word character by character. We have observed that this type of model can be more effective and beneficial than other elementary approaches like String Matching (Cotterell et al., 2017) etc.

For the Word-Ordering problem, we have worked with only statistical and probabilistic approaches till now and haven't yet incorporated any deep learning based approach in our model. Neural models are state of the art in nearly all Natural Language Processing tasks and have always performed better than statistical and probabilistic approaches. So in future, we wish to experiment with deep learning based approaches as well. One major information we didn't exploit is the dependency relations between the words. We hope to come up with a method to somehow quantify those relations and use those values to calculate an improvised language model score. Also, since a dependency tree can be interpreted as a graph, using graph matching and searching techniques is another dimension we can explore.

References

Regina Barzilay and Kathleen R McKeown. 2005. Sentence fusion for multidocument news summarization. *Computational Linguistics*, 31(3):297–328.

Ryan Cotterell, Christo Kirov, John Sylak-Glassman, Géraldine Walther, Ekaterina Vylomova, Patrick Xia, Manaal Faruqui, Sandra Kübler, David Yarowsky, Jason Eisner, and Mans Hulden. 2017. Conll-sigmorphon 2017 shared task: Universal morphological reinflection in 52 languages. *CoRR*, abs/1706.09031.

George Doddington. 2002. Automatic evaluation of machine translation quality using n-gram co-occurrence statistics. In *Proceedings of the Second International Conference on Human Language Technology Research*, HLT '02, pages 138–145, San Francisco, CA, USA. Morgan Kaufmann Publishers Inc.

Sepp Hochreiter and Jürgen Schmidhuber. 1997. Long short-term memory. *Neural Comput.*, 9(8):1735–1780.

Simon Mille, Anja Belz, Bernd Bohnet, Yvette Graham, Emily Pitler, and Leo Wanner. 2018. The First Multilingual Surface Realisation Shared Task (SR'18): Overview and Evaluation Results. In *Proceedings of the 1st Workshop on Multilingual Surface Realisation (MSR), 56th Annual Meeting of the Association for Computational Linguistics (ACL)*, pages 1–10, Melbourne, Australia.

Joakim Nivre, Marie-Catherine de Marneffe, Filip Ginter, Yoav Goldberg, Jan Hajic, Christopher D Manning, Ryan T McDonald, Slav Petrov, Sampo Pyysalo, Natalia Silveira, et al. 2016. Universal dependencies v1: A multilingual treebank collection. In *LREC*.

Kishore Papineni, Salim Roukos, Todd Ward, and Wei-Jing Zhu. 2002. Bleu: A method for automatic evaluation of machine translation. In *Proceedings of the 40th Annual Meeting on Association for Computational Linguistics*, ACL '02, pages 311–318, Stroudsburg, PA, USA. Association for Computational Linguistics.

Ehud Reiter and Robert Dale. 1997. Building applied natural language generation systems. *Natural Language Engineering*, 3(1):57–87.

Andreas Stolcke. 2002. Srilm – an extensible language modeling toolkit. In *IN PROCEEDINGS OF THE 7TH INTERNATIONAL CONFERENCE ON SPOKEN LANGUAGE PROCESSING (ICSLP 2002*, pages 901–904.

Akhilesh Sudhakar and Anil Kumar Singh. 2017. Experiments on morphological reinflection: Conll-2017 shared task. In *Proceedings of the CoNLL SIGMORPHON 2017 Shared Task: Universal Morphological Reinflection*, pages 71–78. Association for Computational Linguistics.

Kelvin Xu, Jimmy Ba, Ryan Kiros, Kyunghyun Cho, Aaron Courville, Ruslan Salakhudinov, Rich Zemel, and Yoshua Bengio. 2015. Show, attend and tell: Neural image caption generation with visual attention. In *International Conference on Machine Learning*, pages 2048–2057.

Surface Realization Shared Task 2018 (SR18): The Tilburg University Approach

Thiago Castro Ferreira and **Sander Wubben** and **Emiel Krahmer**

Tilburg center for Cognition and Communication (TiCC)

Tilburg University

The Netherlands

{tcastrof,s.wubben,e.j.krahmer}@tilburguniversity.edu

Abstract

This study describes the approach developed by the Tilburg University team to the shallow track of the Multilingual Surface Realization Shared Task 2018 (SR18). Based on Castro Ferreira et al. (2017), the approach works by first preprocessing an input dependency tree into an ordered linearized string, which is then realized using a statistical machine translation model. Our approach shows promising results, with BLEU scores above 40 for 4 different languages in development and test sets (English, French, Italian and Spanish) and above 30 for the Dutch and Portuguese languages. The model is publicly available[1].

1 Introduction

This study presents the approach developed by the Tilburg University team for the shallow track of the Multilingual Surface Realization Shared Task 2018 (SR18) (Mille et al., 2018). Given a lemmatized dependency tree without word order information, the goal of this task consists of linearizing the lemmas in the correct order and realizing them as a surface string with the proper morphological form.

For the task, parallel datasets were provided for 10 different languages and we developed our model for 6 out of the 10 languages (Dutch, English, French, Italian, Portuguese, Spanish). We started from the surface realization approach described in Castro Ferreira et al. (2017), where a semantic graph structure is first preprocessed into a preordered linearized form, which is subsequently converted into text using a statistical machine translation model implemented in Moses (Koehn et al., 2007). However for this shared task, instead of a semantic structure, our current approach preprocesses the lemmas of the dependency tree into an ordered linearized version.

Although for the task sufficient parallel corpus data, pairing dependency tree inputs to textual outputs, were made available to train and test our approach, alignments between the source lemmas and the target words were not provided. Since this information is crucial to train our approach, we implemented a method consisting of four consecutive strategies to obtain the alignments.

Except for two languages (Dutch and Portuguese, ironically), our approach showed promising results, with BLEU scores higher than 40 in development and test sets. In the remainder of this paper, we describe the method in more detail: Section 2 explains the alignment method, Section 3 describes the general approach, Section 4 describes the results and discussion of our approach in development and test sets and, finally, Section 5 concludes the study, also describing future work which can be done to improve the model.

2 Alignment

To train and test the models for multilingual surface realization, parallel corpora pairing lemmatized dependency trees and their textual realizations were made available in 10 different languages. However, no word alignments between the two sides were provided, which is a crucial information to train part of our approach. So, to obtain this information, we implemented four sequential alignment strategies.

Before applying these strategies, we first used the spaCy software[2] to tokenize, lemmatize and dependency parse the target texts. Since spaCy

---

[1] https://github.com/ThiagoCF05/Dep2Text

[2] https://spacy.io/

Proceedings of the First Workshop on Multilingual Surface Realisation, pages 35–38

Melbourne, Australia, July 19, 2018. ©2018 Association for Computational Linguistics

only provides models for 6 out of the 10 covered languages, the approach described in this study is limited to these six. For the Portuguese language, we also parsed the contractions between preposition and determiners (e.g., *da/do* and *na/no*, corresponding to *of the* and *in the* in English) into two single tokens (*de a/de o* and *em a/em o* for the previous examples).

Once the target texts were preprocessed, the first step simply compares the lemmas of the source side with the words on the target side. If a lemma on the source side and a word on the target side matched with each other and not with any other element, they were aligned.

In the second step, we applied the same comparison used in the first step, but now for the lemmas of the target words. If lemmas on source and target sides only matched each other and no other element, the source lemma was aligned to the corresponding target word.

The third step aimed to solve situations where a source lemma matches more than one element on the other side, by aligning the source and target lemmas with the same dependency tags which only matched each other.

Finally, the fourth step matched the remaining source and target lemmas of a parallel instance with the shortest string distance.

Based on the alignment between source and target sides of a parallel instance, we trained our approach, as described in the following section.

3 Model

Our model is based on the NLG approach introduced in Castro Ferreira et al. (2017), where a semantic graph structure is first preprocessed into a preordered linearized form, which is then converted into its textual counterpart using a statistical machine translation model implemented with Moses. However for this task, instead of a semantic structure, our approach takes as input a lemmatized dependency tree. In the next sections, we explain the preprocessing and translation phases in more detail.

3.1 Preprocessing

The preprocessing method consists of two steps: linearization and partial realization.

Linearization   aims to linearize a dependency tree input without punctuation nodes into an ordering string format. Our approach is similar to the 2-step classifier introduced in Castro Ferreira et al. (2017). Its pseudo-code is depicted in Algorithm 1.

The approach starts by deciding which first-order child nodes are most likely to be before and after its head node (lines 1-13). It uses a maximum entropy classifier ϕ_1, trained for each language based on the relevant aligned training set. As features, this classifier uses the lemmas as well as the dependency and part-of-speech tags of the head and child nodes.

Once the nodes are split into a group of nodes before and another group of nodes after their heads, each one of these groups is ordered with an algorithm similar to the MergeSort one (lines 14-24 and function $SORT$). To decide the order of two child nodes of a same group, we use a second maximum entropy classifier ϕ_2, also trained for each language based on the corresponding aligned training set. As features (line 44), it uses the lemmas as well as the dependency and part-of-speech tags of the head and the two child nodes involved in each comparison.

Partial realization   aims to partially realize the lemmas in the linearized representation. For each language, it uses a lexicon created based on the aligned information extracted from the datasets, as explained in Section 2. Given a lemma and its features, our approach looks for the most likely morphological form in the lexicon.

3.2 Translation

For each one of the 6 languages which our approach covers, we built a phrase-based machine translation model using the Moses toolkit (Koehn et al., 2007). The MT model aims to convert a linearized dependency tree generated during the preprocessing step into text, adding the proper punctuation marks.

Most of the model settings were copied from the Statistical MT system introduced in Castro Ferreira et al. (2017). At training time, we extract and score phrases up to the size of nine tokens. As feature functions, we used direct and inverse phrase translation probabilities and lexical weighting, as well as word, unknown word and phrase penalties. These feature functions were trained using alignments from the training set obtained by MGIZA (Gao and Vogel, 2008) (not by the ones extracted according to Section 2). Model weights were tuned on the development data using 60-batch

Language	BLEU
Dutch	35.26
English	58.92
French	59.28
Italian	50.33
Portuguese	54.76
Spanish	54.88

Table 1: BLEU scores of our approach in the tokenized development sets.

Language	BLEU	DIST	NIST
Dutch	32.28	57.81	8.05
English	55.29	79.29	10.86
French	52.03	55.54	9.85
Italian	44.46	58.61	9.11
Portuguese	30.82	60.70	7.55
Spanish	49.47	51.73	11.12

Table 2: BLEU, DIST and NIST scores of our approach in the original (non-tokenized) test sets.

Algorithm 1 Linearization method

Require: $depTree$
1: **function** LINEAR($root, orderId$)
2:     $before \leftarrow \emptyset$
3:     $after \leftarrow \emptyset$
4:     $edges \leftarrow getEdges(depTree, root)$
5:     **for all** $edge \in edges$ **do**
6:         $node \leftarrow edge.node$
7:         $features_1 \leftarrow f_1(depTree, root, node)$
8:         **if** $\phi_1(features_1) == before$ **then**
9:             $before \leftarrow before \cup node$
10:         **else**
11:             $after \leftarrow after \cup node$
12:         **end if**
13:     **end for**
14:     $before \leftarrow$ SORT($before$)
15:     **for all** $node \in before$ **do**
16:         $orderId \leftarrow$ LINEAR($node, orderId$)
17:     **end for**
18:     $root.orderId \leftarrow orderId$
19:     $orderId \leftarrow orderId + 1$
20:     $after \leftarrow$ SORT($after$)
21:     **for all** $node \in after$ **do**
22:         $orderId \leftarrow$ LINEAR($node, orderId$)
23:     **end for**
24:     **return** $orderId$
25: **end function**
26:
27: **function** SORT($nodes$)
28:     **if** $|nodes| < 2$ **then**
29:         **return** $nodes$
30:     **end if**
31:     $half \leftarrow |nodes|/2$
32:     $end \leftarrow |nodes|$
33:     $nodes_1 \leftarrow$ SORT($nodes[0, half]$)
34:     $nodes_2 \leftarrow$ SORT($nodes[half, end]$)
35:     $ordNodes \leftarrow \emptyset$
36:     **while** $|nodes_1| > 0$ or $|nodes_2| > 0$ **do**
37:         **if** $|nodes_1| == 0$ **then**
38:             $ordNodes \leftarrow ordNodes \cup$ POP($nodes_2$)
39:         **else if** $|nodes_2| == 0$ **then**
40:             $ordNodes \leftarrow ordNodes \cup$ POP($nodes_1$)
41:         **else**
42:             $node_1 \leftarrow$ POP($nodes_1$)
43:             $node_2 \leftarrow$ POP($nodes_2$)
44:             $features_2 \leftarrow f_1(depTree, node_1, node_2)$
45:             **if** $\phi_2(features_2) == before$ **then**
46:                 $ordNodes \leftarrow ordNodes \cup node_1$
47:                 $ordNodes \leftarrow ordNodes \cup node_2$
48:             **else**
49:                 $ordNodes \leftarrow ordNodes \cup node_2$
50:                 $ordNodes \leftarrow ordNodes \cup node_1$
51:             **end if**
52:         **end if**
53:     **end while**
54:     **return** $ordNodes$
55: **end function**
56:
57: LINEAR($depTree.root, 0$)

MIRA (Cherry and Foster, 2012) with BLEU as the evaluation metric. A distortion limit of 6 was used for the reordering models. We used two lexicalized reordering models: a phrase-level (phrase-msd-bidirectional-fe) (Koehn et al., 2005) and a hierarchical-level one (hier-mslr-bidirectional-fe) (Galley and Manning, 2008). At decoding time, we used a stack size of 1000. To rerank the candidate texts, we used a 5-gram language model trained on the EuroParl corpus (Koehn, 2005) using KenLM (Heafield, 2011).

4 Results and Discussion

Table 1 summarizes the BLEU scores we obtained on the tokenized development data for the 6 relevant languages. For all languages (except Dutch) our approach yielded BLEU scores of 50 or higher, with the highest results obtained for French (with a BLEU score of 59).

Table 2 depicts the BLEU, DIST and NIST scores of our approach on the test sets for the 6 target languages. For most languages, the BLEU scores on development and test set are comparable, albeit somewhat lower. The scores for Portuguese, however, are substantially lower, which we explain as follows. In contrast to the results on the development set, computed by the authors for the lowercased tokenized version of the set, the scores on the test, generated by the organizers, computed the metrics comparing the generated texts with the lowercased and non-tokenized gold-standards. Although we parsed the contractions between preposition and determiners in this language to align source and target data (as explained in Section 2), our approach did not generate these contractions. That is the case, for instance, in the sentence *"greve **na** televisão pública francesa"* (i.e., *strike on the French public television*), generated by our model with the parsed contractions: *"greve **em a** televisão pública francesa"*. We assume this problem explain most of the drop in the BLEU score of the test set in comparison with the development one.

The low scores for Dutch in both development and test set might be due to the way non-segmented words of this language were represented on the source side of the datasets, i.e., their units were split by an underscore. During the surface realization process, our approach did not realize this representation in its correct form, as in the case of the sentence *"Mijn **basis_niveau** is flink omhoog gegaan."*, where the correct form of *basis_niveau* is *basisniveau*. This may have negatively affected the performance of our approach.

5 Conclusion

This study described a shallow surface realizer for 6 languages in the Surface Realization Shared Task 2018 (SR18), with promising results. In future work, we aim to fix the problem of non-segmented words in the Dutch language, as well as the contraction generation in the Portuguese one. Moreover, we aim to evaluate the performance of Neural Machine Translation models in comparison with the statistical used here, in the veins of Castro Ferreira et al. (2017) for AMR-to-text.

References

Thiago Castro Ferreira, Iacer Calixto, Sander Wubben, and Emiel Krahmer. 2017. Linguistic realisation as machine translation: Comparing different mt models for amr-to-text generation. In *Proceedings of the 10th International Conference on Natural Language Generation*, pages 1–10. Association for Computational Linguistics.

Colin Cherry and George Foster. 2012. Batch tuning strategies for statistical machine translation. In *Proceedings of the 2012 Conference of the North American Chapter of the Association for Computational Linguistics: Human Language Technolo-gies*, NAACL-HLT'12, pages 427–436, Montreal, Canada. Association for Computational Linguistics.

Michel Galley and Christopher D. Manning. 2008. A simple and effective hierarchical phrase reordering model. In *Proceedings of the 2008 Conference on Empirical Methods in Natural Language Processing*, EMNLP'08, pages 848–856, Honolulu, Hawaii. Association for Computational Linguistics.

Qin Gao and Stephan Vogel. 2008. Parallel implementations of word alignment tool. In *Software Engineering, Testing, and Quality Assurance for Natural Language Processing*, SETQA-NLP'08, pages 49–57, Columbus, Ohio. Association for Computational Linguistics.

Kenneth Heafield. 2011. Kenlm: Faster and smaller language model queries. In *Proceedings of the Sixth Workshop on Statistical Machine Translation*, WMT '11, pages 187–197, Stroudsburg, PA, USA. Association for Computational Linguistics.

Philipp Koehn. 2005. Europarl: A parallel corpus for statistical machine translation. In *MT summit*, volume 5, pages 79–86.

Philipp Koehn, Amittai Axelrod, Alexandra Birch, Chris Callison-Burch, Miles Osborne, and David Talbot. 2005. Edinburgh System Description for the 2005 IWSLT Speech Translation Evaluation. In *International Workshop on Spoken Language Translation*.

Philipp Koehn, Hieu Hoang, Alexandra Birch, Chris Callison-Burch, Marcello Federico, Nicola Bertoldi, Brooke Cowan, Wade Shen, Christine Moran, Richard Zens, Chris Dyer, Ondřej Bojar, Alexandra Constantin, and Evan Herbst. 2007. Moses: Open source toolkit for statistical machine translation. In *Proceedings of the 45th Annual Meeting of the ACL on Interactive Poster and Demonstration Sessions*, ACL'07, pages 177–180, Prague, Czech Republic. Association for Computational Linguistics.

Simon Mille, Anja Belz, Bernd Bohnet, Yvette Graham, Emily Pitler, and Leo Wanner. 2018. The First Multilingual Surface Realisation Shared Task (SR'18): Overview and Evaluation Results. In *Proceedings of the 1st Workshop on Multilingual Surface Realisation (MSR), 56th Annual Meeting of the Association for Computational Linguistics (ACL)*, pages 1–10, Melbourne, Australia.

The OSU Realizer for SRST '18: Neural Sequence-to-Sequence Inflection and Incremental Locality-Based Linearization

David L. King
The Ohio State University
Department of Linguistics
Columbus, Ohio
king.2138@osu.edu

Michael White
The Ohio State University
Department of Linguistics
Columbus, Ohio
mwhite@ling.osu.edu

Abstract

Surface realization is a nontrivial task as it involves taking structured data and producing grammatically and semantically correct utterances. Many competing grammar-based and statistical models for realization still struggle with relatively simple sentences. For our submission to the 2018 Surface Realization Shared Task, we tackle the shallow task by first generating inflected wordforms with a neural sequence-to-sequence model before incrementally linearizing them. For linearization, we use a global linear model trained using early update that makes use of features that take into account the dependency structure and dependency locality. Using this pipeline sufficed to produce surprisingly strong results in the shared task. In future work, we intend to pursue joint approaches to linearization and morphological inflection and incorporating a neural language model into the linearization choices.

1 Introduction

We participated in the surface track of the 2018 Surface Realization Shared Task (Mille et al., 2018, SRST '18). In the surface track, task inputs were created by extracting sentences in 10 languages from the Universal Dependency treebanks corpus, scrambling the words and converting them to their citation form. The task was then to generate a natural and semantically adequate sentence by inflecting and ordering the words.

Our aims in participating in the shared task were twofold. First, we aimed to investigate the extent to which neural sequence-to-sequence models developed for the 2016 and 2017 SIGMOR-PHON shared tasks on morphological reinflection (Faruqui et al., 2016; Kann and Schütze, 2016) could be adapted to the more realistic setting for generation of SRST '18. Second, we aimed to investigate the extent to which dependency locality (Gibson, 2000) features previously shown to be important for grammar-based generation in English (White and Rajkumar, 2012) and in corpus-based studies of syntactic choice (Temperley, 2007; Liu, 2008; Gildea and Temperley, 2010; Rajkumar et al., 2016) would also prove effective with incremental, dependency-based linearization (Liu et al., 2015; Puduppully et al., 2016) across languages.

At an overview level, our system treats the task of surface realization as a simple two-stage process. First, we convert uninflected lexemes to fully inflected wordforms using the grammatical features supplied by the UD corpus; and second, we incrementally linearize the inflected words using the supplied syntactic dependencies, grammatical features and locality-based features that take dependency length and phrase size into account. A simple rule-based detokenizer attaches punctuation to adjacent words in a final step. The system was trained using only the supplied data. We leave for future work investigating ways to jointly make inflection and linearization choices and to incorporate a neural language model.

2 Background

The intuition behind using neural and statistical models for learning morphology originated with what Ackerman et al. (2009) referred to as the *Paradigm Cell Filling Problem* (PCFP). For any given learner, human or machine, there exists no input such that exposing the learner to that input will also expose the learner to every possible inflected wordform. Nevertheless, humans can rou-

Proceedings of the First Workshop on Multilingual Surface Realisation, pages 39–48
Melbourne, Australia, July 19, 2018. ©2018 Association for Computational Linguistics

Person	Singular	Plural
1st	ich singe	???
2nd	du singst	???
3rd	???	sie singen

Person	Singular	Plural
1st	???	wir hören
2nd	???	ihr hört
3rd	er/sie/es hört	???

Table 1: For SRST '18, our hypothesis is that our system will not see every fully inflected word form in the training data. For example, given partial paradigms for the German verbs for SINGEN ('to sing') and HÖREN ('to hear'), we should have enough information for our system to learn the paradigm of TRINKEN, given only its citation form.

tinely and accurately fill in paradigm tables for wordforms they may have never even produced before. For any language learner, the PCFP states that a learner must take incomplete input (as seen in Table 1) and be able to produce fully inflected paradigm tables for novel words (e.g. Table 2).

Person	Singular	Plural
1st	ich trinke	wir trinken
2nd	du trinkst	ihr trinkt
3rd	er/sie/es trinkt	sie trinken

Table 2: The inferred paradigm for TRINKEN ('to drink') as learned by the partial paradigms for SINGEN ('to sing') and HÖREN ('to hear') from Table 1.

There has been extensive work computationally to combat the PCFP (Nicolai et al., 2015; Durrett and DeNero, 2013) and multiple shared tasks (Cotterell et al., 2016, 2017). Recently, models utilizing recurrent neural networks have proven most effective at the PCFP and have produced state-of-the-art results in the last two SIGMORPHON shared tasks (Kann and Schütze, 2016). Although we think this approach lends itself to our task, in that we need to produce fully inflected wordforms along with linearizing them, Kann and Schütze's system has only been tested on SIGMORPHON data and, to our knowledge, has never been used in a downstream task such as surface realization.

Turning now to dependency locality, Rajku-

mar et al. (2016) provide an overview of the literature on how locality considerations affect syntactic choice in human language production. The tendency to minimize dependency length has a long history of study going back to Behaghel's (1932) principle of end weight. More recently, Hawkins (1994; 2004) and Gibson (2000) have advanced theories contending that ease of production and comprehension favors a preference for dependency locality, bolstered not only by the corpus studies cited earlier but also a wide range of experimental studies. Rajkumar et al. (2016) additionally demonstrate a significant preference for dependency locality in syntactic choice even in the presence of strong controls for surprisal and memory depth. In Section 6, we show that the features we designed to capture locality preferences yield impressive gains on automatic metric scores across languages in the context of our incremental linearization system.

3 Morphological Inflection

As an initial stage in our realization process, we first predict the fully inflected wordforms from the supplied lexemes. We inflect the morphological forms before linearization in order to allow the surface forms to be used as features for linearization, but acknowledge that these steps would ideally be done jointly. For English, a high resource language, morphological inflection is relatively simple to do with existing rule-based resources like MorphG.[1] To predict fully inflected word forms in other languages as well, we exploit recent advances in neural machine translation (NMT) as implemented by Kann and Schütze in the two most recent SIGMORPHON shared tasks. Their system is based on Bahdanau et al.'s (2014) attention-based NMT architecture and models the task of wordform prediction as a kind of *translation* of one sequence to another.

Figure 1 shows the original architecture developed by Faruqui et al. (2016). Given Kann and Schütze's success in adapting this architecture to work with the SIGMORPHON data, we adopt their architecture hypothesizing that it will generalize to the SRST '18 data. The architecture uses gated recurrent units (Chung et al., 2015, GRU), a kind of recurrent neural network, whose hidden state h_t depends on the current input x_t, the previous hidden state h_{t-1}, and nonlinear function f

---

[1] https://github.com/knowitall/morpha

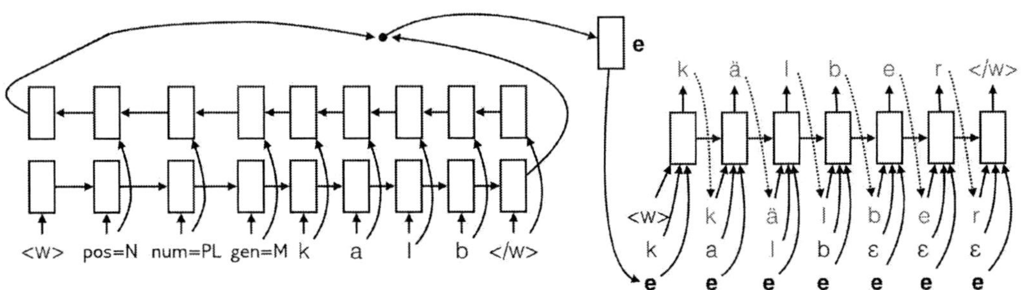

Figure 1: A graphical representation of the architecture originally introduced by Faruqui et al. (2016) and adapted by Kann and Schütze (2016) to handle SIGMORPHON2016 input. A bidirectional GRU creates an encoding of the input wordform and supplied features. That encoding is subsequently fed to the decoder GRU along with the original input wordform.

at time t. Similarly, context c for a given sequence is defined as the output from nonlinear function q over all the hidden states from time step 1 to t over the length of sequence x.

$$h_t = f(x_t, h_{t-1}) \tag{1}$$

$$c = q(h_1, ..., h_{T_x}) \tag{2}$$

Since we used a bidirectional GRU, we set h_j to be the the concatenated vectors of the forwards and backwards encoding of the sequence:

$$h_j = \left[\overrightarrow{h_j^T}, \overleftarrow{h_j^T} \right]^T \tag{3}$$

We define inference (the decoding step) of output y given input sequence x as a distribution of possible output strings:

$$p(y|x) = \prod_{t=1}^{T_y} p(y_t | \{y_1, ..., y_t - 1\}, s_t, c_t) \tag{4}$$

This distribution is derived from the product of previous individual outputs y_1, y_2, ..., y_{t-1} up to the current time step t to produce the most likely output y_t. Output y is also dependent on s_t (the hidden state of the decoder) and context c_t (the weighted sum of annotations produced by the encoder):

$$c_i = \sum_{j=1}^{T_x} \alpha_{ij} h_j \tag{5}$$

Where we calculate weights α_{ij} for h_j as:

$$\alpha_{ij} = \frac{exp(e_{ij})}{\sum_{k=1}^{T_x} exp(e_{ik})} \tag{6}$$

$$e_{ij} = a(s_{i-1}, hj) \tag{7}$$

We used standard cross-entropy loss, 300 hidden units for both the encoder and decoder. We followed Kann and Schütze by training the model using minibatches of 20 and Adadelta (Zeiler, 2012). For the datasets, we used the entirety of the supplied training data, but only used a random sample of 6000 items from the development set to speed up training. Models for each language were trained until wordform prediction accuracy on the development set was over 98% or up to 30 epochs with early stopping. Dropout was set to 0.5.

Table 3 shows our system's performance in selecting fully inflected wordforms on the development set. We also supply two competing baselines as a point of comparison: one in which our system just copies the citation form supplied and one where it only selects the most common inflected wordform seen in training. By and large, we see tremendous improvements in selecting the correct wordform.

Our final feature set included any features supplied by the data, in addition to features from immediate children and parents in the dependency tree. We made use of all features from a given

Model	Language									
	ar	cs	en	es	fi	fr	it	nl	pt	ru
Lemma	11.5	32.9	67.0	45.5	24.9	48.9	50.8	62.9	51.5	6.2
Majority	50.7	43.0	67.5	59.2	26.2	58.5	58.9	65.1	60.3	34.1
MED	92.3	91.7	89.2	99.2	98.6	98.3	92.1	88.5	96.1	90.1

Table 3: Morphological inflection results on the development set compared to baseline results of simply copying the lemma or using the most frequent inflected wordform.

word and any features from any parent word. We also chose to exclusively add features from children with argument relations (i.e. *dobj, nsubj, csubj*, etc.), with the intuition that, for example, the argument of a verb would influence a given verb's inflection, while an adverb might not. To illustrate this, as seen in Figure 2, in the fragment DIT IS MOOI ... ('That is beautiful'), the features from DIT facilitate properly inflecting the verb ZIJN ('to be') as IS ('is') and not BENT or BEN ('are' or 'am' respectively), since the feature 'Person=3' is not encoded in the copula, but rather in the pronoun. Meanwhile the *advmod* relation is not helpful in informing our system how to inflect ZIJN.

Dit is mooi ...

Figure 2: An example (from the Dutch training set) of how child dependencies with argument relations help with inflection, while other modifier relations do not. The person features in DIT help to realize ZIJN as IS and not BENT or BEN. However, the features from the *advmod* relation are not helpful.

4 Linearization

Previous work on dependency-based surface realization (Bangalore and Rambow, 2000; Filippova and Strube, 2007, 2009; Guo et al., 2008; Bohnet et al., 2010, 2011; Guo et al., 2011; Zhang and Clark, 2015) has emphasized bottom-up approaches that make relatively little use of dependency locality. For this task, we opted to follow Liu et al. (2015); Puduppully et al. (2016) in taking an incremental approach to linearization so as to be compatible with future work incorporating neural language models (Wen et al., 2015; Dušek and Jurcicek, 2016; Konstas et al., 2017) while giving greater emphasis to locality considerations.

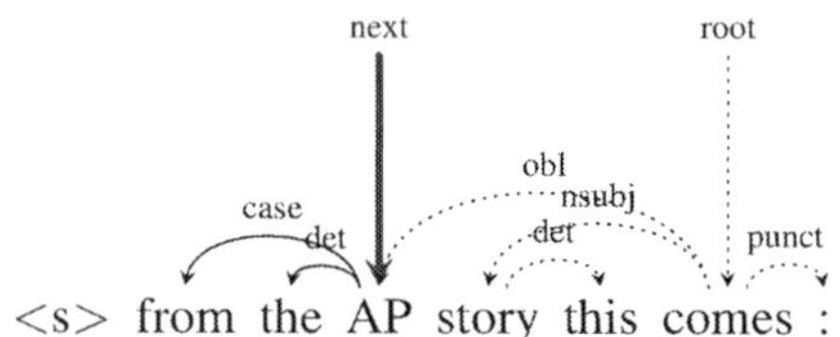

Figure 3: Example candidate realization, with *AP* as the next word and remaining words (with dotted dependencies) still in the randomized input order.

In our approach, a candidate realization is a (partial) permutation of the input words. Candidates are generated by extending a previous candidate with an input word that has not yet been chosen, as illustrated in Figure 3. Since the number of candidates is factorial in the number of input words, beam search is employed with scores computed using a global linear model. By tracking the way in which the input words are permuted, features can be calculated both from the candidate sequence as well as from the input dependency tree.

To further constrain linearization choices, projective outputs can be enforced by ensuring that all output phrases are continuous. To do so, we calculate the successors of the previous word and require the next word choice to be a descendant of one of the successors. If the previous word has child words in the dependency tree that have not yet been linearized, then the successors are the as-yet-unselected children. Otherwise, the successors include the unrealized parent and siblings of the previous word; if all those words have been covered, successors are calculated by recursing up the tree.

Since we found that 2.5% of the English development trees contained non-projective trees (even ignoring punctuation as a source of discontinuity), we opted to allow non-projective outputs to be generated. To do so, we used a discontinuity feature to encourage the model to learn that most choices should yield continuous phrases,

Events	Base Predictors	Locality Predictors
next word	trigram word, stem and POS	
dependency ordering	whether initial or final; parent and child stems, POSs, grammatical features and dep relation; sibling stem, POS and dep rel	difference in log binned size of sibling subtree
completed arc	whether projective; parent and child stems, POSs and dep relation	log binned dependency length
discontinuity	trigram POS; bigram dep relation; relation of extraposed dep	log binned size of extraposed subtree

Table 4: Linearization features, which combine events with different base and locality predictors.

where the next word is taken to introduce a discontinuity if it is not a descendant of the previous word's successors. A benefit of this soft approach to enforcing projectivity is that all sequences can be generated in principle. Note that our approach to calculating successors is similar to (though simpler than) the aforementioned transition-based approaches while also allowing limited non-projectivity.

We used scikit-learn's implementation[2] of the passive-aggressive classifier (Crammer et al., 2006) for our global linear model. The model was trained discriminatively using early update with the additional requirement that the gold candidate be top-ranked in the beam (Puduppully et al., 2016). Mini-batches were processed in parallel by averaging the updated models. To encourage faster training, we averaged the models after each mini-epoch of only a few mini-batches, rather than waiting to the end of an entire training epoch. Nevertheless, we suspect that the models were undertrained as training often failed to reach the end of longer sentences even after 12 hours of training using between 12 and 28 processors (not all languages were given 28 processors to obtain faster throughput). Looking at the training curve for English, we obtained good performance after 10 epochs but the BLEU score on the development set was still generally increasing when training timed out at 30 epochs.

Our feature set is summarized in Table 4. Features are based on four kinds of events that are calculated as each word is added: next-word events, dependency-ordering events, completed-arc events and discontinuity events. A variety of predictors are extracted for each kind of event, as shown in the table. Base features include

trigram word-, POS- and stem-sequences, parent and child stems, dependency relations, parent and child grammatical features, and whether a word is initial or final in its phrase. Locality-based features additionally include binned dependency length for completed arcs, binned difference in size of sibling subtrees and binned size of any extraposed dependent subtree. For lookahead, ancestor ordering features are calculated in the same way as the head-dependent ordering features, so for example starting a sentence with a determiner entails that its head noun will precede its parent (e.g. the main verb). Features are count-based and constructed by combining each event with each of its predictors and each pair of two predictors. For example, when adding *AP* in Figure 3 as the next word, one of the constructed features pairs the previous two POS tags with the next-word event as `next_word=AP:prev2_pos=IN:prev_pos=DT` and its count is incremented.

For ease of implementation, we limited the model to count-based features. By contrast, in previous work with a bottom-up, chart-based realizer, White and Rajkumar (2012) found it helpful to include a feature whose value was the total dependency length of a constituent. In the incremental setting here, we expect that the binned relative size of siblings is the most helpful locality-based feature for ordering, as the binned dependency length feature likely does not become available in a timely fashion in the beam search with long dependencies. In future work, we plan to investigate ways to better model the total dependency length incrementally by accumulating the sum of open dependencies in candidate realizations.

| **BLEU** | | | | | **Language** | | | | | |
	ar	cs	en	es	fi	fr	it	nl	pt	ru
NoLoc	27.5	47.5	56.8	57.9	33.1	34.6	36.7	23.5	44.1	45.8
Dev	29.3	53.7	68.9	65.0	35.9	38.4	42.3	26.2	48.0	56.6
Test	25.6	53.2	66.3	65.3	37.5	38.2	42.1	25.5	47.6	57.9
DIST										
NoLoc	40.1	53.6	66.1	53.5	55.8	51.9	51.0	47.7	74.3	51.9
Dev	42.7	58.1	71.9	62.9	56.3	55.0	55.1	47.4	73.5	58.9
Test	46.7	58.1	70.2	61.5	58.7	53.7	59.7	57.8	66.0	59.9
NIST										
NoLoc	7.39	13.0	11.4	12.1	9.18	8.64	8.54	7.27	8.92	13.6
Dev	7.50	13.4	12.2	12.7	9.40	8.90	8.92	7.45	9.24	14.1
Test	7.15	13.5	12.0	12.7	9.56	8.00	8.70	7.33	9.13	14.2

Table 5: Automatic metric results for combined system on development and test sets, along with ablation results with no locality features (NoLoc) for the dev set.

5   Results

Many of our results were turned in late because of library compatibility issues: in particular, since Kann and Schütze's code is based on an outdated version of Theano, which is difficult to support, we could not port the morphology inflection system to more powerful computing clusters and were thus limited to training on a single unit with only one GPU. Nevertheless, we were careful to perform no further development after the deadline, and the organizers encouraged us to submit results for all of the languages when we could.

Automatic metric results for the combined morphological inflection and linearization system (with rule-based detokenizer) appear in Table 5, along with no-locality ablation results discussed in the next section. Results for the development and test sets were fairly consistent across all three automatic metrics used in the shared task. Based on the test results shared with the participants, our combined system was among the top performers for all languages, with particularly strong BLEU results for Arabic, Czech, Spanish, Finnish, Portuguese and Russian (French, Italian and Dutch may have suffered from undertrained linearization models). Metric scores varied widely across the languages, though the variation was largely consistent with that observed by other participants, suggesting that some languages are more challenging than others for surface realization (or at least more difficult to achieve high metric scores with).

6   Analysis and Discussion

6.1   Morphological Inflection

Compared to previous work in the context of the SIGMORPHON shared tasks, the SRST '18 input and output vocabulary for the morphological inflection system was much larger. Having a larger search space seems to have affected languages non-uniformly. Although we have different feature sets, Spanish and Russian seem to be unaffected where as Dutch and English scores are drastically lower than expected.

At the actual sub-word level, sequence to sequence models are unable to take account of context originating from outside the input sequence. For example, we observe that the model frequently confuses when to use English 'a' and 'an', since the information necessary to make this prediction does not occur within the character sequence for the word. In future work, an architecture that jointly performs linearization and morphological inflection could address this issue.

Another error type seen at the sub-word level is that although the system learns what affixes look like in a given language, it does not always learn exactly how to apply them, as often seen with Russian. For example, when the system should produce UCHENYJ ('scientist)' and instead produces UCHENOGO, it is confusing the adjectival ending of -OGO for the nominal ending -YJ, both of which however mean masculine, singular, and genitive.

	Language									
	ar	cs	en	es	fi	fr	it	nl	pt	ru
Rate	8.25	12.3	2.43	9.21	7.04	4.11	5.16	8.96	10.6	7.16
Recall	16.2	16.9	16.7	13.8	9.57	6.00	3.45	35.7	18.6	26.9
Precision	25.0	62.0	47.1	44.7	52.9	15.8	25.0	34.9	68.8	23.8

Table 6: Non-projective dependency prevalence, recall and precision in the development set.

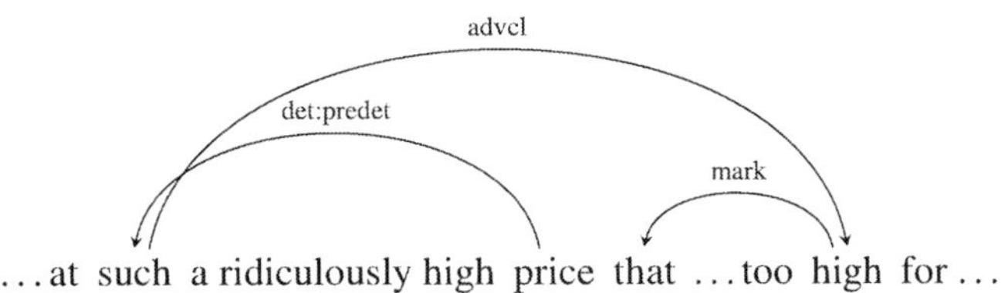

Figure 4: Example from the development set where a non-projective adverbial clause dependency from *such* to *high* is successfully reproduced, enhancing fluency.

6.2 Linearization

To examine the impact of the dependency locality features, we trained an ablated model with no locality features and compared its performance on the development set to the full model, as shown in Table 5. The ablated model performed worse for all languages with BLEU & NIST, and for most languages with DIST. Moreover, the locality-based features achieved impressive gains in BLEU scores ranging between 2 and 12 points, with the most dramatic gains for Spanish, Russian and English.

We also investigated whether the full model better approximated the total dependency length of the gold development sentences than the ablated model, but the results were inconclusive, with the full model coming closer to gold for some languages but not others. With better incremental features for modeling total dependency length, we plan to investigate in future work whether locality-based features can indeed better match the gold total dependency length in an incremental setting, as found in our earlier work with a bottom-up, chart-based realizer (White and Rajkumar, 2012). Nevertheless, we did find many examples such as the one in Table 7 where the locality-based features helped to ameliorate search errors. In the table, the realization using the ablated model (NoLoc) fails to linearize the dependents *al Sadr - 's* anywhere near their head *Muqtada*, mistakenly leaving them till the end of the sentence where they contribute to a much higher total dependency length than in the

gold sentence (Gold) or the realization using the full model (Dev). Note that the full model does not correctly order the name *Muqtada al-Sadr* either, but the realization is still much easier to interpret as intended. As an aside, the realization also includes another local ordering error, *before only three months*; we expect that incorporating a neural language model in future work will resolve many problems of this kind.

Turning now to non-projectivity, we found that sentences with extraposed phrases like those in the gold sentences were sometimes successfully generated. Table 6 shows that the percentage of sentences in the development set with at least one non-projective dependency ranged from a low of 2.5% for English to over 12% for Czech.[3] Recall of the gold non-projective dependencies was generally low, while precision was generally more reasonable, reaching 62% for Czech. Restricting outputs to be projective generally led to small decreases in BLEU scores on the development set, with English and Czech seeing the largest drops of 1.5 and 3.3 points, respectively, though Finnish and Russian witnessed improvements of nearly 1 BLEU point. An example illustrating the successful realization of a non-projective dependency appears in Figure 4; by contrast, if only projective dependencies are allowed, the best possible realization would still be the quite unnatural ...*at a*

---

[3]A dependency between a head and its dependent was considered projective if all the intervening words (ignoring punctuation tokens) in the linearized sequence were descendants of the head.

Gold: the Coalition decision to provoke a fight with <u>Muqtada al - Sadr 's movement</u> only three months before the Coaliti on Provisional Authority goes out of business has to be seen as a form of gross incompetence in governance . (deplen 84)

NoLoc: the Coalition decision to provoke a fight with <u>Muqtada movement</u> before three months only the Provisional Coalition Authority goes out of business has to be seen as a form of gross incompetence in governance . <u>al Sadr - 's</u> (deplen 144)

Dev: the Coalition decision to provoke a fight with <u>Muqtada - Sadr al 's movement</u> before only three months the Coalition Provisional Authority goes out of business has to be seen as a form of gross incompetence in governance . (deplen 90)

Table 7: Example from the development set showing how locality-based features help ameliorate search errors (with total dependency length in parentheses).

ridiculously high price such that . . . .

7 Conclusion

We have shown surprisingly competitive results by modeling realization as a two-stage process where we first generate morphologically inflected wordforms using a neural sequence-to-sequence model and then incrementally linearize those wordforms using a global linear model. We additionally show that NMT systems, which have been producing state-of-the-art results in morphological reinflection, can be generalized and integrated into other tasks. We also find that dependency structure and dependency locality are highly informative in the linearization step and allow us to also generate some cases of non-projectivity. In future work, we intend to pursue coupling the learning of morphological inflection and linearization into a single process and using a neural language model to help with linearization choices.

Acknowledgments

We thank Micha Elsner for helpful comments and discussion. This work was supported in part by NSF grants IIS-1319318 and IIS-1618336. The work was also supported by an allocation of computing time from the Ohio Supercomputer Center.

References

Farrell Ackerman, James P Blevins, and Robert Malouf. 2009. Parts and wholes: Implicative patterns in inflectional paradigms. *Analogy in grammar: Form and acquisition*, pages 54–82.

Dzmitry Bahdanau, Kyunghyun Cho, and Yoshua Bengio. 2014. Neural machine translation by jointly learning to align and translate. *arXiv preprint arXiv:1409.0473*.

Srinivas Bangalore and Owen Rambow. 2000. Exploiting a probabilistic hierarchical model for generation. In *Proc. COLING-00*.

Otto Behaghel. 1932. *Deutsche Syntax: eine geschichtliche Darstellung. Band IV. Wortstellung. Periodenbau.* Heidelberg: Carl Universitatsbuchhandlung, Germany.

Bernd Bohnet, Simon Mille, Benoît Favre, and Leo Wanner. 2011. Stumaba : From deep representation to surface. In *Proceedings of the 13th European Workshop on Natural Language Generation*, pages 232–235. Association for Computational Linguistics.

Bernd Bohnet, Leo Wanner, Simon Mill, and Alicia Burga. 2010. Broad coverage multilingual deep sentence generation with a stochastic multi-level realizer. In *Proceedings of the 23rd International Conference on Computational Linguistics (Coling 2010)*, pages 98–106. Coling 2010 Organizing Committee.

Junyoung Chung, Caglar Gulcehre, Kyunghyun Cho, and Yoshua Bengio. 2015. Gated feedback recurrent neural networks. In *International Conference on Machine Learning*, pages 2067–2075.

Ryan Cotterell, Christo Kirov, John Sylak-Glassman, Géraldine Walther, Ekaterina Vylomova, Patrick Xia, Manaal Faruqui, Sandra Kübler, David Yarowsky, Jason Eisner, and Mans Hulden. 2017. CoNLL-SIGMORPHON 2017 Shared Task: Universal morphological reinflection in 52 languages. *CoRR*, abs/1706.09031.

Ryan Cotterell, Christo Kirov, John Sylak-Glassman, David Yarowsky, Jason Eisner, and Mans Hulden. 2016. The SIGMORPHON 2016 Shared Task— Morphological Reinflection. In *Proceedings of the 2016 Meeting of SIGMORPHON*, Berlin, Germany. Association for Computational Linguistics.

Koby Crammer, Ofer Dekel, Joseph Keshet, Shai Shalev-Shwartz, and Yoram Singer. 2006. Online passive-aggressive algorithms. *Journal of Machine Learning Research*, 7:551–585.

Greg Durrett and John DeNero. 2013. Supervised learning of complete morphological paradigms. In *HLT-NAACL*, pages 1185–1195.

Ondřej Dušek and Filip Jurcicek. 2016. Sequence-to-sequence generation for spoken dialogue via deep syntax trees and strings. In *Proceedings of the 54th Annual Meeting of the Association for Computational Linguistics (Volume 2: Short Papers)*, pages 45–51. Association for Computational Linguistics.

Manaal Faruqui, Yulia Tsvetkov, Graham Neubig, and Chris Dyer. 2016. Morphological inflection generation using character sequence to sequence learning. In *Proc. of NAACL*.

Katja Filippova and Michael Strube. 2007. Generating constituent order in German clauses. In *ACL 2007, Proceedings of the 45th Annual Meeting of the Association for Computational Linguistics, June 23-30, 2007, Prague, Czech Republic*. The Association for Computer Linguistics.

Katja Filippova and Michael Strube. 2009. Tree linearization in English: Improving language model based approaches. In *Proceedings of Human Language Technologies: The 2009 Annual Conference of the North American Chapter of the Association for Computational Linguistics, Companion Volume: Short Papers*, pages 225–228, Boulder, Colorado. Association for Computational Linguistics.

Edward Gibson. 2000. Dependency locality theory: A distance-based theory of linguistic complexity. In Alec Marantz, Yasushi Miyashita, and Wayne O'Neil, editors, *Image, Language, brain: Papers from the First Mind Articulation Project Symposium*. MIT Press, Cambridge, MA.

Daniel Gildea and David Temperley. 2010. Do grammars minimize dependency length? *Cognitive Science*, 34(2):286–310.

Yuqing Guo, Josef van Genabith, and Haifeng Wang. 2008. Dependency-based n-gram models for general purpose sentence realisation. In *Proc. COLING-08*.

Yuqing Guo, Deirdre Hogan, and Josef van Genabith. 2011. Dcu at generation challenges 2011 surface realisation track. In *Proceedings of the 13th European Workshop on Natural Language Generation*, pages 227–229. Association for Computational Linguistics.

John A. Hawkins. 1994. *A Performance Theory of Order and Constituency*. Cambridge University Press, New York.

John A. Hawkins. 2004. *Efficiency and Complexity in Grammars*. Oxford University Press.

Katharina Kann and Hinrich Schütze. 2016. MED: The LMU system for the SIGMORPHON 2016 shared task on morphological reinflection. *ACL 2016*, page 62.

Ioannis Konstas, Srinivasan Iyer, Mark Yatskar, Yejin Choi, and Luke Zettlemoyer. 2017. Neural amr: Sequence-to-sequence models for parsing and generation. In *Proceedings of the 55th Annual Meeting of the Association for Computational Linguistics (Volume 1: Long Papers)*, pages 146–157. Association for Computational Linguistics.

Haitao Liu. 2008. Dependency distance as a metric of language comprehension difficulty. *Journal of Cognitive Science*, 9(2):159–191.

Yijia Liu, Yue Zhang, Wanxiang Che, and Bing Qin. 2015. Transition-based syntactic linearization. In *Proceedings of NAACL*, Denver, Colorado, USA.

Simon Mille, Anja Belz, Bernd Bohnet, Yvette Graham, Emily Pitler, and Leo Wanner. 2018. The First Multilingual Surface Realisation Shared Task (SR'18): Overview and Evaluation Results. In *Proceedings of the 1st Workshop on Multilingual Surface Realisation (MSR), 56th Annual Meeting of the Association for Computational Linguistics (ACL)*, pages 1–10, Melbourne, Australia.

Garrett Nicolai, Colin Cherry, and Grzegorz Kondrak. 2015. Inflection generation as discriminative string transduction. In *Proceedings of the 2015 Conference of the North American Chapter of the Association for Computational Linguistics: Human Language Technologies*, pages 922–931. Association for Computational Linguistics.

Ratish Puduppully, Yue Zhang, and Manish Shrivastava. 2016. Transition-based syntactic linearization with lookahead features. In *Proceedings of the 2016 Conference of the North American Chapter of the Association for Computational Linguistics: Human Language Technologies*, pages 488–493, San Diego, California. Association for Computational Linguistics.

Rajakrishnan Rajkumar, Marten van Schijndel, Michael White, and William Schuler. 2016. Investigating locality effects and surprisal in written English syntactic choice phenomena. *Cognition*, 155:204–232.

David Temperley. 2007. Minimization of dependency length in written English. *Cognition*, 105(2):300–333.

Tsung-Hsien Wen, Milica Gasic, Nikola Mrkšić, Pei-Hao Su, David Vandyke, and Steve Young. 2015. Semantically conditioned lstm-based natural language generation for spoken dialogue systems. In *Proceedings of the 2015 Conference on Empirical Methods in Natural Language Processing*, pages 1711–1721. Association for Computational Linguistics.

Michael White and Rajakrishnan Rajkumar. 2012. Minimal dependency length in realization ranking. In *Proceedings of the 2012 Joint Conference on Empirical Methods in Natural Language Processing and Computational Natural Language Learning,* pages 244–255, Jeju Island, Korea. Association for Computational Linguistics.

Matthew D Zeiler. 2012. Adadelta: an adaptive learning rate method. *arXiv preprint arXiv:1212.5701*.

Yue Zhang and Stephen Clark. 2015. Syntax-based word ordering using learning-guided search. *Computational Linguistics*, 41(3).

Generating High-Quality Surface Realizations Using Data Augmentation and Factored Sequence Models

Henry Elder
ADAPT Centre,
Dublin City University, Ireland
henry.elder@adaptcentre.ie

Chris Hokamp
Aylien Ltd.
Dublin, Ireland
chris@aylien.com

Abstract

This work presents state of the art results in reconstruction of surface realizations from obfuscated text. We identify the lack of sufficient training data as the major obstacle to training high-performing models, and solve this issue by generating large amounts of synthetic training data. We also propose preprocessing techniques which make the structure contained in the input features more accessible to sequence models. Our models were ranked first on all evaluation metrics in the English portion of the 2018 Surface Realization shared task.

1 Introduction

Contextualized Natural Language Generation (NLG) is a long-standing goal of Natural Language Processing (NLP) research. The task of generating text, conditioned on knowledge about the world, is applicable to almost any domain. However, despite recent advances on some tasks, NLG models still produce relatively low quality outputs in many settings. Representing the context in a consistent manner is still a challenge: how can we condition output on a stateful structure such as a graph or a tree?

Several shared tasks have recently explored NLG from inputs with graph-like structures; RDF triples (Colin et al., 2016), dialogue act-based meaning representations (Novikova et al., 2017) and abstract meaning representations (May and Priyadarshi, 2017). In each of these challenges, the input has structure beyond simple linear sequences; however, to date, the top results in these tasks have consistently been achieved using relatively standard sequence-to-sequence models.

The **surface realization** task (Mille et al., 2018) is a conceptually simple challenge: given shuffled input, where tokens are represented by their lemmas, parts of speech, and dependency features, can we train a model to reconstruct the original text? A model that performs well at this task is likely to be a good starting point for solving more complex tasks, such as NLG from Resource Description Framework (RDF) graphs or Abstract Meaning Representation (AMR) structures. In addition, training data for the surface realization task can also be generated in a fully-automated manner.

In this work, we show that training dataset size may be the major obstacle preventing current sequence-to-sequence models from doing well at NLG from structured inputs. Although inputting the structures themselves is theoretically appealing (Tai et al., 2015), for some tasks it may be enough to use sequential inputs by flattening structures, and providing structural information via input factors, as long as the training dataset is sufficiently large. By augmenting training data using a large corpus of unannotated data, we obtain a new state of the art in the surface realization task using off-the-shelf sequence to sequence models.

In addition, we show that information about the output word order, implicitly available in the universal dependency fields, provides essential information about the word order of correct output sequences, confirming that structural information cannot be discarded without a large drop in performance.

The main contributions of this work are:

1. We show how training datasets can be augmented with synthetic data

2. We apply preprocessing steps to simplify the universal dependency structures, making the structure more explicit

Proceedings of the First Workshop on Multilingual Surface Realisation, pages 49–53
Melbourne, Australia, July 19, 2018. ©2018 Association for Computational Linguistics

3. We evaluate copy attention models for the surface realization task

2 The Surface Realization Shared Task

In the **shallow** track of the 2018 surface realization (SR) shared task, inputs consist of tokens from a universal dependency (UD) tree provided in the form of lemmas. The original order of the sequence is obfuscated by random shuffling[1].

Models are evaluated on their ability to reconstruct the original, unshuffled input which generated the features. In order to do this, models must make use of structural information in order to reorder the tokens correctly as well as part-of-speech and/or dependency parse labels in order to restore the correct surface realization of lemmas. Note that we focus upon the English sub-task, where word order is critical because of the typologically analytic nature of English, however, for other languages, restoring word order may be less important, while deriving surface realizations from lemmas may be much more challenging.

3 Datasets

3.1 Augmenting Training with Synthetic Datasets

To augment the SR training data, we used sentences from the WikiText corpus (Merity et al., 2016). Each of these sentences was parsed using UDPipe (Straka and Straková, 2017) to obtain the same features provided by the SR organizers. We then filtered this data, keeping only sentences with at least 95% vocabulary overlap with the in-domain SR training data. Note that the input vocabulary for this task is word lemmas, so at least 95% of the tokens in each instance in our additional training data are lemmas which are also found in the in-domain data. The order of tokens in each instance of this additional dataset is then randomly shuffled to simulate the random input order in the SR data.

We thus obtain 642,960 additional training instances, which are added to the 12,375 instances supplied by the SR shared task organizers.

---

[1] The task organizers also introduced a **deep** task, but since ours was the only submission to the deep task, we save our discussion of this task for future work.

4 Features

4.1 Leveraging Structured Features

Because we have the dependency parse features for each input, some (noisy) information about word order is implicitly available from the parse information; however, discovering the structural relationship between the dependency parse features and the order of words in the output sequence is likely to be challenging for our sequence to sequence model. Therefore, we re-construct the original parse tree from the dependency features, and perform a depth-first search to sort and reorder the lemmas. This is similar to the linearization step performed by Konstas et al. (2017), the main difference being we randomly choose between child nodes instead of using a predetermined order based on edge types.

In order to further augment the available context, we experiment with adding potential delemmatized forms for each input lemma. The possible forms for each lemma were found by creating a map from $(\textbf{lemma}, \textbf{xpos}) \rightarrow \textbf{form}$, using the WikiText dataset. For each input lemma and xpos, we then check for the pair in the map – if it exists, the corresponding form is appended to the sequence. This makes forms available to the model for copying.

For some $(\textbf{lemma}, \textbf{xpos})$ pairs there are multiple potential forms. When this occurs we add all potential forms to the input sequence. The mapping was found to cover 98.9% of cases in the development set.

4.2 Factored Inputs

Factored models were introduced by Alexandrescu et al. (2006) as a means of including additional features beyond word tokens into neural language models. The key idea is to create a separate embedding representation for each feature type, and to concatenate the embeddings for each input token to create its dense representation. Sennrich et al. (2016) showed that this technique is quite effective for neural machine translation, and some recent work, such as Hokamp (2017) has successfully applied this technique to related sequence generation tasks.

The embedding e_j for each input token x_j with

FEATURE	DESCRIPTION	VOCABULARY SIZE	EMBEDDING SIZE
lemma	the lemma of the surface word	30004	300
XPOS	the English part-of-speech label	53	16
position	the position in the sequence	103	25
UPOS	the universal part-of-speech label	20	8
head position	the position of the head word according to the dependency parser	100	25
deprel	the dependency relation label according to the dependency parser	51	15

Table 1: The features used in the factored models, along with the number of possible values the feature may take, and the respective embedding size.

POSITION	LEMMA	XPOS	UPOS	HEAD POSITION	DEPREL
1	learn	VERB	VB	2	acl
2	lot	NOUN	NN	4	nsubj
3	there	PRON	EX	4	expl
4	be	VERB	VBZ	0	root
5	about	ADP	IN	8	case
6	a	DET	DT	2	det
7	.	PUNCT	.	4	punct
8	Chernobyl	PROPN	NNP	1	obl
9	to	PART	TO	1	mark

Table 2: An example from the training data, containing all features we use as input factors.

factors F is created as in Eq. 1:

$$e_j = \prod_{k=1}^{|F|} \mathbf{E}_k x_{jk} \qquad (1)$$

where $\|$ indicates vector concatenation, $\mathbf{E}_k$ is the embedding matrix of factor k, and x_{jk} is a one hot vector for the k-th input factor. Table 1 lists each of the factors used in our models, along with its corresponding embedding size. The embedding size of 300 for the lemma is set in configuration, while the embedding sizes of the other features are set heuristically by OpenNMT-py, using the heuristic $|embedding_k| = |V_k|^{0.7}$, where $|V_k|$ is the vocabulary size of feature k. Table 2 gives an example from the training data with actual instantiations of each of the features.

5 Model

Models were trained using the OpenNMT-py toolkit (Klein et al., 2017). The model architecture is a 1 layer bidirectional recurrent neural network (RNN) with long short-term memory (LSTM) cells (Hochreiter and Urgen Schmidhuber, 1997) and attention (Luong et al., 2015). The model has 450 hidden units in the encoder and decoder layers, and 300 hidden units in the word embeddings which are learned jointly across the whole model. Dropout of 0.3 is applied between the LSTM stacks. We use a coverage attention layer (Tu et al., 2016) with lambda value of 1.

The models are trained using stochastic gradient descent with learning rate 1. A learning rate decay of 0.5 is applied at each epoch once perplexity does not decrease on the validation set. Models were trained for 20 epochs. Output was decoded using beam search with beam size 5. Unknown tokens were replaced with the input token that had the highest attention value at that time step. The approach of copying input tokens using attention is commonly known as a pointer network (Vinyals et al., 2015). Output from the epoch checkpoint which performed best on the development set was chosen for test set submission.

The exploration and choice of hyperparameters was aided by the use of Bayesian hyperparameter optimization platform SigOpt[2].

6 Experiments

We experiment with many different combinations of input features and training data, in order to understand which elements of the representation have the largest impact upon performance.

We limit vocabulary size during training to enable the network to generalize to unknown tokens at test time. When using just the SR training data we train word embeddings for the 15,000 most frequent tokens from a possible 23,650 unique tokens. When using the combined SR training data and filtered WikiText dataset we use the 30,000 most frequent tokens from a possible 106,367 unique tokens.

We trained on a single Tesla K40 GPU. Training time was approximately 1 minute per epoch for the SR data and 1 hour per epoch for the combined SR data and filtered WikiText.

7 Results

We report results using automated evaluation metric BLEU (Papineni et al., 2002). On the test set we additionally report the NIST (Przybocki et al., 2009) score and the normalized edit distance (DIST).

SYSTEM	BLEU
SR Baseline	21.27
SR + delemma suggestions	23.75
SR + delemma suggestions + linearization	43.11
SR + delemma suggestions + linearization + additional data	68.86

Table 3: Ablation study with BLEU scores for different configurations on the shallow task development set

Table 3 presents the results of the surface realization experiments. We observe three main components that drastically improve performance over the baseline model:

1. augmenting the training set with more data

2. reordering the input using the dependency parse features

3. providing potential forms via the delemmatization map

Table 4 gives the official SR 2018 results from task organizers. Our system, which corresponds to the best configuration from Table 3 was ranked first across all metrics.

TEAM ID	BLEU	DIST	NIST
1 (Ours)	**69.14**	**80.42**	**12.02**
2	28.09	70.01	9.51
3	8.04	47.63	7.71
4	66.33	70.22	**12.02**
5	50.74	77.56	10.62
6	55.29	79.29	10.86
7	23.2	51.87	8.86
8	29.6	65.9	9.58
AVG	41.3	67.86	10.15

Table 4: Official results of the surface realization shared task using BLEU, DIST and NIST as evaluation metrics.

8 Related Work

The surface realization task bears the closest resemblance to the SemEval 2017 shared task AMR-to-text (May and Priyadarshi, 2017). Our approach to data augmentation and preprocessing uses many insights from Neural AMR (Konstas et al., 2017). Traditional data-to-text systems use a rule based approach (Reiter and Dale, 2000).

9 Conclusion

The main takeaway from this work is that data augmentation improves performance on the surface realization task. Although unsurprising, this result confirms that sufficient data is needed to achieve reasonable performance, and that flattened structural information such as dependency parse features is insufficient without additional preprocessing to reduce the complexity of the input. The surface realization task is ostensibly quite simple, thus it is surprising that baseline sequence to sequence models, which perform well in other tasks such as machine translation, cannot solve this task. We hypothesize that the lemmatization and shuffling of the input does not provide sufficient information to reconstruct the input. In sequences longer than a few words, there is likely to be significant ambiguity without additional structural in-

[2]https://sigopt.com/

formation such as parse features. However, reconstructing the original sequence from unprocessed, flattened parse information alone is unrealistic using standard encoder-decoder models.

In future work, we plan to explore more challenging variants of this task, while also experimenting with models that do not require feature-specific preprocessing to make use of rich structural information in the input.

References

Andrei Alexandrescu and Katrin Kirchhoff. 2006. Factored neural language models. In *Proceedings of the Human Language Technology Conference of the NAACL, Companion Volume: Short Papers*. Association for Computational Linguistics, Stroudsburg, PA, USA, NAACL-Short '06, pages 1–4. http://dl.acm.org/citation.cfm?id=1614049.1614050.

Emilie Colin, Claire Gardent, M Yassine, and Shashi Narayan. 2016. The WebNLG Challenge : Generating Text from DBPedia Data. *The 9th International Conference on Natural Language Generation* .

Sepp Hochreiter and J Urgen Schmidhuber. 1997. Long Short-Term Memory. *Neural Computation* 9(8):1735–1780. https://doi.org/10.1162/neco.1997.9.8.1735.

Chris Hokamp. 2017. Ensembling factored neural machine translation models for automatic post-editing and quality estimation. In *Proceedings of the Second Conference on Machine Translation*. Association for Computational Linguistics, pages 647–654. http://aclweb.org/anthology/W17-4775.

Guillaume Klein, Yoon Kim, Yuntian Deng, Josep Crego, Jean Senellart, and Alexander M. Rush. 2017. OpenNMT: Open-source Toolkit for Neural Machine Translation pages 67–72. https://doi.org/10.18653/v1/P17-4012.

Ioannis Konstas, Srinivasan Iyer, Mark Yatskar, Yejin Choi, and Luke Zettlemoyer. 2017. Neural AMR: Sequence-to-Sequence Models for Parsing and Generation https://doi.org/10.1145/nnnnnnn.nnnnnnn.

Minh-Thang Luong, Hieu Pham, and Christopher D. Manning. 2015. Effective Approaches to Attention-based Neural Machine Translation https://doi.org/10.18653/v1/D15-1166.

Jonathan May and Jay Priyadarshi. 2017. SemEval-2017 Task 9: Abstract Meaning Representation Parsing and Generation. *SemEval* pages 536–545. http://nlp.arizona.edu/SemEval-2017/pdf/ScmEval090.pdf.

Stephen Merity, Caiming Xiong, James Bradbury, and Richard Socher. 2016. Pointer Sentinel Mixture Models http://arxiv.org/abs/1609.07843.

Simon Mille, Anja Belz, Bernd Bohnet, Yvette Graham, Emily Pitler, and Leo Wanner. 2018. The First Multilingual Surface Realisation Shared Task (SR'18): Overview and Evaluation Results. In *Proceedings of the 1st Workshop on Multilingual Surface Realisation (MSR), 56th Annual Meeting of the Association for Computational Linguistics ({ACL})*. Melbourne, Australia, pages 1–10.

Jekaterina Novikova, OndÅŹej Dušek, and Verena Rieser. 2017. The E2E Dataset: New Challenges For End-to-End Generation (August):201–206. http://arxiv.org/abs/1706.09254.

Kishore Papineni, Salim Roukos, Todd Ward, and Wei-Jing Zhu. 2002. BLEU: A Method for Automatic Evaluation of Machine Translation. In *Proceedings of the 40th Annual Meeting on Association for Computational Linguistics*. Association for Computational Linguistics, Stroudsburg, PA, USA, ACL '02, pages 311–318. https://doi.org/10.3115/1073083.1073135.

Mark Przybocki, Kay Peterson, SÃľbastien Bronsart, and Gregory Sanders. 2009. The NIST 2008 Metrics for machine translation challenge—overview, methodology, metrics, and results. *Machine Translation* 23(2):71–103. https://doi.org/10.1007/s10590-009-9065-6.

Ehud Reiter and Robert Dale. 2000. *Building Natural Language Generation Systems*. Cambridge University Press, New York, NY, USA.

Rico Sennrich and Barry Haddow. 2016. Linguistic input features improve neural machine translation. In *Proceedings of the First Conference on Machine Translation, WMT 2016, colocated with ACL 2016, August 11-12, Berlin, Germany*. pages 83–91. http://aclweb.org/anthology/W/W16/W16-2209.pdf.

Milan Straka and Jana Straková. 2017. Tokenizing, POS Tagging, Lemmatizing and Parsing UD 2.0 with UDPipe. In *Proceedings of the CoNLL 2017 Shared Task: Multilingual Parsing from Raw Text to Universal Dependencies*. Association for Computational Linguistics, Vancouver, Canada, pages 88–99. http://www.aclweb.org/anthology/K/K17/K17-3009.pdf.

Kai Sheng Tai, Richard Socher, and Christopher D. Manning. 2015. Improved Semantic Representations From Tree-Structured Long Short-Term Memory Networks pages 1556–1566. https://doi.org/10.1515/popets-2015-0023.

Zhaopeng Tu, Zhengdong Lu, Yang Liu, Xiaohua Liu, and Hang Li. 2016. Modeling Coverage for Neural Machine Translation https://doi.org/10.1145/2856767.2856776.

Oriol Vinyals, Meire Fortunato, and Navdeep Jaitly. 2015. Pointer Networks http://arxiv.org/abs/1506.03134.

AX Semantics' Submission to the Surface Realization Shared Task 2018

Andreas Madsack, Johanna Heininger, Nyamsuren Davaasambuu,

Vitaliia Voronik, Michael Käufl, and **Robert Weißgraeber**

AX Semantics, Stuttgart, Germany
`{firstname.lastname}@ax-semantics.com`

Abstract

In this paper we describe our system and experimental results on the development set of the Surface Realisation Shared Task (Mille et al., 2017). Our system is an entry for Shallow-Task, with two different models based on deep-learning implementations for building the sentences combined with a rule-based morphology component. We trained our systems on all 10 given languages.

1 Introduction

This paper describes our approach for the First Multilingual Surface Realisation Shared Task (Mille et al., 2018). For the surface task the dependency parse trees were given unordered and the words lemmatized. The objective was to order the words in the sentences and to inflect the given lemmas. The data was provided in 10 languages: English, Spanish, French, Portuguese, Italian, Dutch, Czech, Russian, Arabic, and Finnish.

Our aim was to build new deep learning based ordering systems, augmented by using our already implemented (rule-based) morphology for the inflection part. System 1 implemented the initial idea and system 2 followed after mediocre results in system 1.

Final scoring for the MSR shared task was using System 2.

2 Linearization

Here we propose two systems: both are implemented using Keras (Chollet et al., 2015) and Tensorflow (Abadi et al., 2016), are trained using each language from the CoNLL data sets separately and finally also trained with all languages combined. These two systems, however, differ in their internal models (see the following two sections).

To generate training data the given training CoNLL data sets were matched to their corresponding original data using tree based matching. Each node was compared based on `deprel`, `lemma/form`, `upostag`, and number of children in a recursive manner traversing the tree from top to bottom.

2.1 System 1: Sequence-to-Sequence Model

System 1 is a new approach using sequence-to-sequence models (Vinyals et al., 2016), encoder-decoder, and attention as described in Bahdanau et al. (2014) for machine translation. Instead of using LSTM cells, we used bidirectional GRU cells (Cho et al., 2014). Some early stage evaluations showed GRU converges better than LSTM for this task.

The input sequence is an unordered list of words and their features; the features for each word consist of: `id`, `upostag`, `deprel`, `head-id`, `head-upostag`, `head-deprel`, and `level` in the syntax-tree. All features are encoded in embeddings. The embeddings are shared between the two matching fields (i.e. `deprel` and `head-deprel`). Figure 1 shows a visualization of the model.

The result of the sequence model is a sequence of correct positions of the words for a complete sentence. This order, together with the given lemma and features from the data set, is then processed by a morphology component, which also takes care of building the "final readable sentence" including e.g. capitalization.

We trained two sub-models for each language with the sequence lengths of 25 and 400. We chose these values based on the length of the sentences in the training data set – the 75% quantile is at length 25 which includes most of the sentences. 400 is the absolute maximal length of sentences (the longest sentence has 398 words and is

54

Proceedings of the First Workshop on Multilingual Surface Realisation, pages 54–57
Melbourne, Australia, July 19, 2018. ©2018 Association for Computational Linguistics

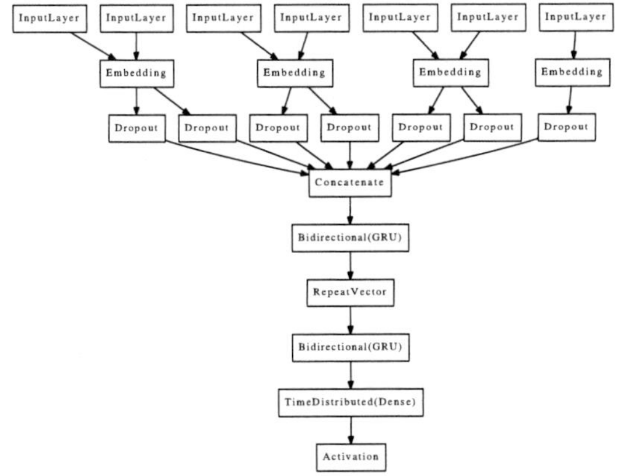

Figure 1: Sequence-to-Sequence Model
The inputs are: (id, head-id), (upos, head-upos), (deprel, head-deprel), (level)

in Arabic). We used 0 value padding for sequences shorter than the maximum given by the model.

These two sub-models are then available for the prediction phase, during which the model is chosen by the length of input sentence being shorter than that of the next fitting model. The predicted sequence probabilities are selected so that every word appears only once in the final sentence.

Automatic evaluation of the dev-set resulted in BLEU scores and DIST scores given in table 1. We used the evaluation code given by the shared task organizers. This evaluation step includes the morphology described in section 3. We used the matching model for the language and a model trained with all languages.

lang	BLEU (language)	BLEU (ALL)	DIST (language)	DIST (ALL)
en	0.020	0.019	0.124	0.133
es	0.007	0.007	0.071	0.071
fr	0.009	0.009	0.094	0.096
pt	0.012	0.013	0.106	0.107
it	0.007	0.008	0.095	0.098
nl	0.010	0.013	0.099	0.102
cs	0.009	0.011	0.082	0.085
ru	0.009	0.007	0.073	0.076
ar	0.002	0.003	0.071	0.072
fi	0.010	0.012	0.083	0.084

Table 1: Scores for Sequence-to-Sequence Model (development data)

2.2 System 2: Pairwise Classification

The second system is a classification model that calculates the word ordering by estimating if word1 is right of word2. Each word of a sen-

tence is calculated against every other word in the same sentence. Features used in training for each of the two words are upostag, deprel, head-upostag, head-deprel and level in the syntax-tree. Same as System 1 the embeddings are shared between the two matching fields.

The predicted word1-is-right-of-word2 probabilities are used for each subtree to find the order. On the next level the subtree is ordered by the probability of the head node of the subtree.

The results show that particularly upostag=PUNCT is now mostly at the end of sentences even for commas and other punctuations. Human inspection results in a positively increased overall readability of the output compared to the Sequence-to-Sequence Model (our System 1). See table 2 for results on the given dev-set.

Like the Sequence-to-Sequence model, we have evaluated this model using the matching language and a model trained on all languages.

lang	BLEU (language)	BLEU (ALL)	DIST (language)	DIST (ALL)
en	0.205	0.175	0.430	0.354
es	0.100	0.139	0.182	0.273
fr	0.154	0.137	0.190	0.308
pt	0.153	0.137	0.314	0.308
it	0.105	0.106	0.309	0.258
nl	0.161	0.123	0.298	0.270
cs	0.099	0.110	0.279	0.235
ru	0.239	0.142	0.260	0.245
ar	0.044	0.059	0.163	0.199
fi	0.078	0.064	0.197	0.223

Table 2: Scores for Pairwise Classification Model (development data)

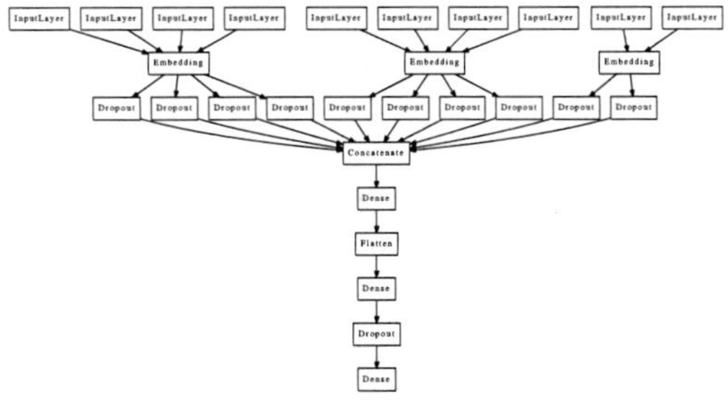

Figure 2: Pairwise Classification Model
The inputs are: (w1-upos, w1-head-upos, w2-upos, w2-head-upos), (w1-deprel, w1-head-upos, w2-deprel, w2-head-upos), (w1-level, w2-level)

Reference	From the AP comes this story:
System 1	Comes from story this AP the:
System 2	This story comes from the AP:
Reference	I took my Mustang here and it looked amazing after they were done, they did a great job, I'm very satisfied with the results.
System 1	With results job I my took satisfied it amazing here did very Mustang. great I, they were a are after looked done the, and they
System 2	I took here Mustang my looked it amazing after they done were and they did a great job I are very satisfied the with results,,.
Reference	Lopulta saatiin halikuva otettua
System 1	Sadaan lopulta ottattua halikuva.
System 2	Lopulta sadaan ottattua halikuva.
Reference	Pastrana begon een politiek offensief om de Copa voor Colombia te behouden.
System 1	Voor beginde. offensief te politiek een Pastrana Colombia Copa om behouden de
System 2	Pastrana om behouden te Copa de voor Colombia beginde offensief een politiek.

Table 3: Example outputs

3 Morphologization

The morphology step employs the NLG system from AX Semantics (Weißgraeber and Madsack, 2017). That system is rule-based and for each inflection request it runs through a decision chain, in which all parts of speech and corresponding grammatical features of the specific languages are implemented.

For irregular words the AX Semantics NLG system uses lexicon entries, which always supercede the rule-based inflection. Grammatical features like number, case, animacy and tense are implemented in a general way, then added to each language alongside its individual configuration.

Since the CoNLL features differ from our usual input parameters, some preprocessing was necessary to map the terms accordingly. The words were also cleaned with regard to special characters like hash tags or diacritics before they were processed by the NLG morphology component.

The accuracy of the morphology component was tested separately on the dev-set for each language. Results are summarized in table 4. Most of the languages show a decent accuracy score of over 90%, whereas Arabic and Finnish with their more complicated morphology still achieve around 80%.

The table also shows that for some languages the accuracy scores for verbs are significantly lower than for nouns or adjectives. For example, in case of Dutch this happens mainly because a given lemma is not the infinitive form as expected from our system but a finite verb form (3rd person singular) and first has to be transformed to the infinitive. This can largely be attributed to the specialization of the system for the language of commerce, which results in a partial under-coverage

language	nouns	adjectives	verbs	mean
en	0.90	0.92	0.93	0.94
es	0.94	0.96	0.86	0.94
fr	0.94	0.93	0.81	0.94
pt	0.91	0.95	0.79	0.95
it	0.94	0.95	0.77	0.93
nl	0.86	0.86	0.50	0.90
cs	0.82	0.91	0.88	0.91
ru	0.92	0.91	0.60	0.90
ar	0.73	0.69	0.40	0.81
fi	0.60	0.65	0.62	0.79

Table 4: Accuracy of the morphology step (examples for single POS categories and mean overall accuracy)

of certain language features for edge cases. We expect coverage to increase as usage expands to more fields.

Furthermore, some of the errors are due to the data being erroneous or incomplete (e.g., only case is given, when number and animacy would also be needed).

4 Conclusion and Future Work

On the whole, none of the systems solve the task satisfactorily.

System 2 shows better scores and somewhat improved readability in contrast to System 1. See table 3 for illustration.

In both linearization systems, we use neither the lemma nor an embedding of the lemma to allow a comparison between the language models and the ALL-language model. This serves as a baseline for comparison against systems where language-specific features can be added.

Our focus for this workshop was to build a linearization system that is simple and does not receive any topic-specific or language-specific input data nor configurations, and without building a neuronal network for morphologization. For pure morphologization tasks, especially for Finnish, Arabic and Hungarian with a large list of very rare cases, we will improve inflection by adding a NN-based morphology component as well.

References

Martin Abadi, Paul Barham, Jianmin Chen, Zhifeng Chen, Andy Davis, Jeffrey Dean, Matthieu Devin, Sanjay Ghemawat, Geoffrey Irving, Michael Isard, Manjunath Kudlur, Josh Levenberg, Rajat Monga, Sherry Moore, Derek G. Murray, Benoit Steiner, Paul Tucker, Vijay Vasudevan, Pete Warden, Martin Wicke, Yuan Yu, and Xiaoqiang Zheng. 2016. Tensorflow: A system for large-scale machine learning. In *12th USENIX Symposium on Operating Systems Design and Implementation (OSDI 16)*, pages 265–283.

Dzmitry Bahdanau, Kyunghyun Cho, and Yoshua Bengio. 2014. Neural machine translation by jointly learning to align and translate. *CoRR*, abs/1409.0473.

Kyunghyun Cho, Bart van Merrienboer, Çaglar Gülçehre, Fethi Bougares, Holger Schwenk, and Yoshua Bengio. 2014. Learning phrase representations using RNN encoder-decoder for statistical machine translation. *CoRR*, abs/1406.1078.

François Chollet et al. 2015. Keras. `https://keras.io`.

Simon Mille, Anja Belz, Bernd Bohnet, Yvette Graham, Emily Pitler, and Leo Wanner. 2018. The First Multilingual Surface Realisation Shared Task (SR'18): Overview and Evaluation Results. In *Proceedings of the 1st Workshop on Multilingual Surface Realisation (MSR), 56th Annual Meeting of the Association for Computational Linguistics (ACL)*, pages 1–10, Melbourne, Australia.

Simon Mille, Bernd Bohnet, Leo Wanner, and Anja Belz. 2017. Shared task proposal: Multilingual surface realization using universal dependency trees. In *Proceedings of the 10th International Conference on Natural Language Generation*, pages 120–123. Association for Computational Linguistics.

Oriol Vinyals, Samy Bengio, and Manjunath Kudlur. 2016. Order matters: Sequence to sequence for sets. In *International Conference on Learning Representations (ICLR)*.

Robert Weißgraeber and Andreas Madsack. 2017. A working, non-trivial, topically indifferent nlg system for 17 languages. In *Proceedings of the 10th International Conference on Natural Language Generation*, pages 156–157. Association for Computational Linguistics.

NILC-SWORNEMO at the Surface Realization Shared Task: Exploring Syntax-Based Word Ordering using Neural Models

Marco A. S. Cabezudo and **Thiago A. S. Pardo**
Interinstitutional Center for Computational Linguistics (NILC)
Institute of Mathematical and Computer Sciences, University of São Paulo
São Carlos - SP, Brazil
`msobrevillac@usp.br, taspardo@icmc.usp.br`

Abstract

This paper describes the submission by the NILC Computational Linguistics research group of the University of São Paulo/Brazil to the Track 1 of the Surface Realization Shared Task (SRST Track 1). We present a neural-based method that works at the syntactic level to order the words (which we refer by NILC-SWORNEMO, standing for "Syntax-based Word ORdering using NEural MOdels"). Additionally, we apply a bottom-up approach to build the sentence and, using language-specific lexicons, we produce the proper word form of each lemma in the sentence. The results obtained by our method outperformed the average of the results for English, Portuguese and Spanish in the track.

1 Introduction

In recent years, Universal Dependencies[1] (UD) have gained interest from many researchers across different areas of Natural Language Processing (NLP). Currently, there are treebanks for about 50 languages that are freely available[2].

UD treebanks have already proved useful in the development of multilingual applications, becoming an advantage for developers. Thus, the creation of an application for a specific language may be replicable to other languages.

The Surface Realization Shared Task (Mille et al., 2018) aims at continuing with the development of natural language generation methods focused on the surface realization task. In this edition of the task, two tracks were proposed: (1)

Shallow Track, which aimed at ordering the words in a sentence and recovering their correct forms, and (2) Deep Track, which aimed at ordering the words and introducing missing functional words and morphological features.

For building the dataset for the Shallow Track, the UD structures were processed as follows:

- the information on word ordering is removed by randomly scrambling the words;

- the words are replaced by their lemmas.

An example of the input data to this track is shown in Figure 1. In this example, we may see information about lemmas, grammatical categories, inflection information and dependency relations.

Track 1 can be seen as word ordering and inflection generation tasks. Word ordering is a fundamental problem in Natural Language Generation (Reiter and Dale, 2000). This problem have been widely studied, e.g., we may see the works proposed for the Shared Task in Surface Realization (Belz et al., 2011). In relation to this problem, this has been addressed using language modeling (Schmaltz et al., 2016) and syntax-based approaches (Zhang and Clark, 2015). Recently, sequence-to-sequence models have also been used to tackle this problem, obtaining good results (Hasler et al., 2017).

In this paper, we present a neural-based method that works at the syntactic level to order the words (which we refer by NILC-SWORNEMO, standing for "Syntax-based Word ORdering using NEural MOdels", developed by the NILC research group on Computational Linguistics). Additionally, we apply a bottom-up approach to build the sentence and, using language-specific lexicons, we produce the word forms of each lemma in the sentence. Our system is described in Section 2. In Section 3, the results of our proposal are presented. Finally,

---

[1] Available at http://universaldependencies.org/#en
[2] Available at https://lindat.mff.cuni.cz/repository/xmlui/handle/11234/1-1983

Proceedings of the First Workshop on Multilingual Surface Realisation, pages 58–64
Melbourne, Australia, July 19, 2018. ©2018 Association for Computational Linguistics

```
1    replace     VERB   VBG    VerbForm=Ger                      24    advcl       _    _
2    W.          PROPN  NNP    Number=Sing                       7     flat        _    _
3    the         DET    DT     Definite=Def|PronType=Art         28    det         _    _
4    Columbia    PROPN  NNP    Number=Sing                       29    nmod        _    _
5    as          ADP    IN     _                                 12    case        _    _
6    Superior    PROPN  NNP    Number=Sing                       28    compound    _    _
7    Steffen     PROPN  NNP    Number=Sing                       1     obj         _    _
8    term        NOUN   NN     Number=Sing                       24    obl         _    _
9    for         ADP    IN     _                                 8     case        _    _
10   15          NUM    CD     NumType=Card                      15    nummod      _    _
11   Graae       PROPN  NNP    Number=Sing                       7     flat        _    _
12   judge       NOUN   NN     Number=Sing                       8     nmod        _    _
13   ,           PUNCT  ,      _                                 24    punct       _    _
14   Bush        PROPN  NNP    Number=Sing                       24    nsubj       _    _
15   year        NOUN   NN     Number=Sing                       8     compound    _    _
16   -           PUNCT  HYPH   _                                 15    punct       _    _
17   the         DET    DT     Definite=Def|PronType=Art         29    det         _    _
18   a           DET    DT     Definite=Ind|PronType=Art         8     det         _    _
19   Jennifer    PROPN  NNP    Number=Sing                       24    obj         _    _
20   .           PUNCT  .      _                                 24    punct       _    _
21   M.          PROPN  NNP    Number=Sing                       19    flat        _    _
22   Anderson    PROPN  NNP    Number=Sing                       19    flat        _    _
23   of          ADP    IN     _                                 4     case        _    _
24   nominate    VERB   VBD    Mood=Ind|Tense=Past|VerbForm=Fin  0     root        _    _
25   associate   ADJ    JJ     Degree=Pos                        12    amod        _    _
26   of          ADP    IN     _                                 29    case        _    _
27   of          ADP    IN     _                                 28    case        _    _
28   Court       PROPN  NNP    Number=Sing                       12    nmod        _    _
29   District    PROPN  NNP    Number=Sing                       28    nmod        _    _
```

Figure 1: Unordered sentence in CoNLL format - "Bush nominated Jennifer M. Anderson for a 15-year term as associate judge of the Superior Court of the District of Columbia, replacing Steffen W. Graae."

some conclusions and future work are discussed in Section 4.

2   System Description

Our proposal was motivated by the works of (Hasler et al., 2017) and (Zhang and Clark, 2015). Thus, we tackled the problem by applying a syntax-based word ordering strategy using a sequence-to-sequence model (seq-2-seq). This way, we could take advantage of the importance of the syntactic information in the word ordering process (in this case, dependency relations) and the length of the sequence of words to be ordered. Thus, we could try to order sub-trees and then apply a bottom-up approach to compose the original sentence. We have to note that our approach have a limitation related to non-projective tree structures, because the allowed realizations will be generated from the dependency structure.

Additionally, we could benefit from the ability of the seq-2-seq model to deal with short sequences (delimited by the length of words in a syntactic level, i.e., a sub-tree generated by the dependency relations), and the few number of hyperparameters to tune, facilitating the training.

2.1   Data Preparation

As we mentioned, we used a neural model to order the words in the syntactic level, and this kind of model requires several instances to learn. Therefore, the first step was to generate and prepare our dataset.

The dataset used to train our models was composed by the training dataset provided by the task and a portion of the Europarl corpus (Koehn, 2005), comprising approximately 70,000 sentences for each language (English, Portuguese, and Spanish).

As our neural model works on words of a sentence according to their syntactic levels, we had to preprocess the dataset to get the words of each sentence by syntactic level. Thus, we run the UDPipe tool (Straka and Straková, 2017) on the dataset and obtained all the information about lemmas, grammatical categories, and dependency relations. Then, we got all the sub-trees (sub-root and children, only via breadth search) and generated a sequence for each sub-tree.

Each sequence was composed by tokens in the sub-tree and each token had the notation "lemma|POS-Tag|dep", where the POS-Tag is the grammatical category and dep is the name of the dependency relation. Besides, the first token in a sequence contains the word "root" as its dependency relation. We used the POS-Tags and the dependency relations to bring more linguistic information into our models.

An example of a sub-tree may be seen in Figure 2. The returned sequence of this sub-tree was as follows: "term|NOUN|root for|ADP|case judge|NOUN|nmod year|NOUN|compound a|DET|det".

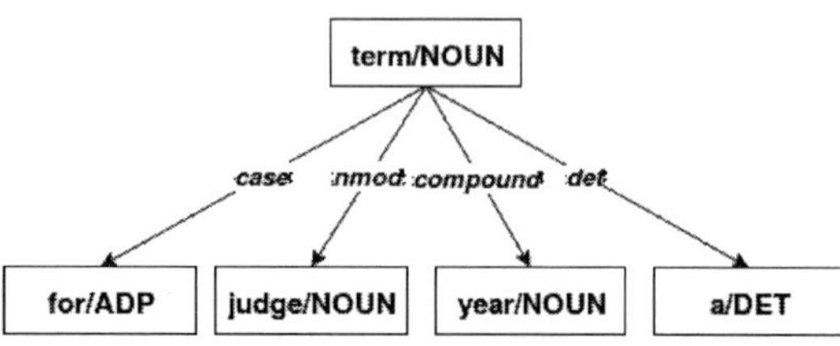

Figure 2: Sub-tree of the sentence that includes "term", "for", "judge", "year", and "a"

One problem related to the training dataset generation was the possibility of the sub-tree's elements to appear in different ordering in the CoNLL format. This would produce different instances, as we build the samples by breadth search in a sub-tree. Thus, we could get the sample "term|NOUN|root *for|ADP|case* judge|NOUN|nmod year|NOUN|compound a|DET|det" or "term|NOUN|root judge|NOUN|nmod year|NOUN|compound for|ADP|case a|DET|det", depending on the order in which they are presented in the CoNLL format, and producing different outputs in our model. This should not be a problem because models have to generalize independently of the order. However, we adopted a strategy to deal with this problem. The strategy was to generate a few permutations for each initial instance of the dataset and join them to build the dataset. We might generate all possible permutations for each initial instance of the dataset, but this would not be good in our case. Instead, we assumed that few permutations would be enough to generalize. Thus, we experimented generating 5, 10 and 15 instances for each instance in the dataset and tested in the neural model. Experiments showed that 5 permutations were enough to achieve a good performance and incrementing to 10 or 15 did not bring improvements.

Finally, it is important to highlight that the lemmas of proper nouns were replaced by the expression "PROPN" in order to reduce data sparsity.

2.2 Word Ordering

The neural model that we used was a sequence-to-sequence model (Encoder-Decoder) (Sutskever et al., 2014) in which the input was composed by a sequence of tokens in a sub-tree extracted by the syntactic dependency relations (described in Subsection 2.1) and the output was composed by the lemmas of the same sequence in the correct order.

In general, each token in the encoder was represented by embeddings composed by the concatenation of the word embedding, the embedding of the grammatical category and the embedding of the dependency relation. We used word embeddings of 300 dimensions provided by GloVe (Pennington et al., 2014) for English[3], Portuguese[4] (Hartmann et al., 2017), and Spanish (built over the corpus provided by Cardellino (2016)). In the case of the other features, we used the number of values that they may assume to generate the size of the embedding.

The type of cells in the Recurrent Neural Network (RNN) that we used was the Long Short-Term Memory (LSTM). We used a Bidirectional LSTM (Bi-LSTM) in the Encoder because it could give us a general understanding of the sentence (saving relations in two directions). In the case of the Decoder, we used two layers and the attention mechanism proposed by Bahdanau et al. (2014) in order to consider all words in the contexts (due to the unordered words). This proposal was similar to the recurrent neural network language model proposed in (Hasler et al., 2017).

Finally, we used a Adam Optimizer with a initial learning rate of 0.001, a dropout value of 0.3, 500 hidden units, 15 epochs, and, for the generation of the sequence, we applied beam search of size 10. Let us mention that we used OpenNMT (Klein et al., 2017) to train our model. These parameters were effective during the training, excepting the number of epochs because we did not try other settings.

2.3 Sentence Building

After the execution of the neural model, we got the words of all sub-trees (obtained by the syntactic levels) in the correct order. In order to build the sentence, we applied a bottom-up approach. Thus, we continuously started to join fragments (belong-

---

[3] Available at https://nlp.stanford.edu/projects/glove/

[4] Available at http://www.nilc.icmc.usp.br/nilc/index.php/ repositorio-de-word-embeddings-do-nilc

ing to sub-trees) with the sub-trees in an immediately higher level until the top of the tree. The joining was performed using the token in common in both sub-trees. For example, in Figure 3, it may be seen the fragment "15 - year" in a sub-tree and the fragment "for a year term judge" in an immediate higher level, where the joining produced the fragment "for a 15 - year term judge".

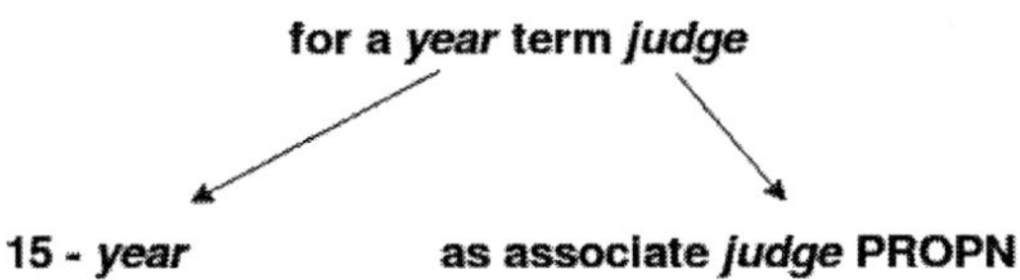

Figure 3: Portion of the ordered sub-trees

As we may see in Figure 3, one of the fragments contains the expression "PROPN". In cases where there was a "PROPN" symbol, our method simply replaced it by the correct proper noun in the original fragment. In other cases, our method had to find the correct place for each proper noun in the fragment. Additionally, there were several cases where the neural model could not obtain all the words in the fragment, mainly in situations where the number of tokens in the input was too long.

To solve these problems, we used a 3-gram language model for English (Chelba et al., 2013), Portuguese (Cunha, 2016) and Spanish (Cardellino, 2016) in order to find the correct position of the words and the proper nouns. That motivated us to follow a bottom-up approach to build a sentence. Thus, the joining between two neighbor syntactic levels makes more sense (as analyzing from the lowest levels brings correct expressions like "15 - year" or "as associate judge", instead of "for a year term judge").

2.4 Inflection Generation

In order to recover the correct words included in a sentence (and not lemmas), we created a lexicon for each language (English, Portuguese and Spanish).

To do this, we ran the UDPipe tool[5] on the Europarl corpus for English, Portuguese and Spanish (Koehn, 2005) in order to get the lemmas and the inflection information. For example, in the sentence "I ran all day", we

got the following information about "ran": "run Mood=Ind|Tense=Past|VerbForm=Fin", which means that "ran" is in indicative mood, in the past tense and in its finite form, and the lemma is "run".

It is important to highlight that we only extracted the inflection information of words that belong to some specific grammatical categories, as auxiliary verbs, verbs, determiners, adjectives, pronouns, and nouns, since these categories usually contain inflection information.

The lexicons generated for English, Portuguese and Spanish contain 44,667, 143,058, and 155,482 entries, respectively. With these lexicons, we executed the last step of our process, the inflection generation. Once the target sentence was ordered, we analyzed each token of the sentence and found its respective inflection word using the appropriate lexicon. It should be noted that there was no preference in inflection selection because we used our lexicon as a hash table, i.e., we were worried about the occurrence of the lemma and the morphological information to get the inflection.

Finally, we applied some rules to handle contractions and other types of problems (as the use of commas).

3 Results and Analysis

The performance of the methods in the Task 1 was computed using the following four metrics:

- BLEU (Papineni et al., 2002): precision metric that computes the geometric mean of the n-gram precisions between the generated text and reference texts, adding a brevity penalty for shorter sentences. We use the smoothed version and report results for n = 1, 2, 3, and 4;

- NIST (Doddington, 2002): related n-gram similarity metric weighted in favor of less frequent n-grams, which are taken to be more informative;

- CIDEr (Vedantam et al., 2015): designed for image description, and similar in spirit to NIST (in that it assigns lower weights to n-grams that are common to the reference texts) (determined by using TF-IDF metric);

- Normalized edit distance (DIST): inverse, normalized, character-based string-edit distance that starts by computing the minimum

---

[5]UDPipe is a trainable pipeline for tokenization, part of speech tagging, lemmatization and dependency parsing of CoNLL files. It contains models for several languages. It is available at http://ufal.mff.cuni.cz/udpipe.

number of character insertions, deletions and substitutions (all at cost 1) required to turn the system output into the (single) reference text.

For now, only the results for BLEU, NIST and DIST have been released. The results of our method for the test data are shown in Table 1, as well as the average results for all the systems that participated in the track. One may see that our method outperformed the average for each language.

Some examples of the results obtained for English, Portuguese and Spanish are shown in Table 2. As we may see, in sentence 1 for English, Portuguese and Spanish, the generated sentences were exactly the same as the reference. This may be explained by the short size of the sentences (excepting for Spanish, whose sentence is not so short).

In sentence 3 for English and 2 and 3 for Spanish, we may see that, even though the results were not correct (in relation to the ordering), some fragments could make sense ("The stocking for my 150 gallon tank is here..." in sentence 3 for English) and, sometimes, texts are still understandable (like sentences 2 and 3 for Spanish), preserving the overall meaning of the sentence.

We could also realize some limitations in our proposal. Firstly, we had some troubles with the software for lexicon building and it was necessary to review and correct some entries. For example, the sentence 2 in English contains the word "v" and the correct word was "have", and the sentence 2 in Portuguese shows the word "levá" and the correct word should be "levar".

Another limitation is related to the number of children in each level of the syntactic tree. In cases where the root of a sub-tree had several children, the seq-to-seq model returned incomplete sequences and the post-processing had more work to do, and, therefore, it usually performed poorly. For example, in sentence 3 for Portuguese, the syntactic tree has "Holland" as root in a level and "Spain", "Itália", "Belgium", ",", "or", and "em" are its children, and the result was not in correct order. Besides, a higher number of punctuations, missing words and proper nouns produced some mistakes in some cases, like sentence 2 for Spanish.

4 Conclusions and Future Work

In this paper, we presented a neural-based surface generation method that works at the syntactic level to order the words. Overall, our method outperformed the average results for English, Portuguese and Spanish. For Portuguese, the language in which we are particularly interested, we produced the best results for the NIST metric (although there is no statistical difference in relation to the system in the second place), and the second best results for BLEU and DIST, which we consider to be very good results.

Among the positive aspects, we noted that our method works fine when the length of the sentence is not too long. Furthermore, even though the results were not correct in some cases (in relation to the ordering), some fragments could make sense and, sometimes, texts were still understandable.

As future work, we may mention the review of the lexicons and possibly the implementation of a better inflection generator. Moreover, we would like to explore algorithms to deal with punctuations in order to improve the performance of our method.

Acknowledgments

The authors are grateful to FAPESP, CAPES and CNPq for supporting this work.

References

Dzmitry Bahdanau, Kyunghyun Cho, and Yoshua Bengio. 2014. Neural machine translation by jointly learning to align and translate. *CoRR*, abs/1409.0473.

Anja Belz, Michael White, Dominic Espinosa, Eric Kow, Deirdre Hogan, and Amanda Stent. 2011. The first surface realisation shared task: Overview and evaluation results. In *Proceedings of the 13th European Workshop on Natural Language Generation*, ENLG '11, pages 217–226, Stroudsburg, PA, USA. Association for Computational Linguistics.

Cristian Cardellino. 2016. Spanish Billion Words Corpus and Embeddings.

Ciprian Chelba, Tomas Mikolov, Mike Schuster, Qi Ge, Thorsten Brants, and Phillipp Koehn. 2013. One billion word benchmark for measuring progress in statistical language modeling. *CoRR*, abs/1312.3005.

Andre Luiz Verucci da Cunha. 2016. Coh-Metrix-Dementia: análise automática de distúrbios de linguagem nas demências utilizando Processamento de Línguas Naturais. Master's thesis, Instituto de

Language	BLEU	NIST	DIST	AVG BLEU	AVG NIST	AVG DIST
English	50.74	10.62	77.56	41.30	10.15	67.86
Portuguese	27.12	7.56	57.43	24.71	7.36	55.30
Spanish	51.58	11.17	53.78	33.66	9.01	35.65

Table 1: Achieved results

Language	Reference	Output
English	(1) Iran says it is creating nuclear energy without wanting nuclear weapons. (2) You have to see these slides....they are amazing. (3) Here is the stocking for my 150 gallon tank i upgraded it to 200 at the weekend because of the clownloach A 200 gallon with 6 pairs of Breeding Angel fish fire mouth honey Gouramis 5 8 inch clownloach a Krib and 5 1 inch clown loach with 16 cory cats 5 Australian Rainbows	(1) Iran says it is creating nuclear energy without wanting nuclear weapons. (2) You *v* to saw these slides.... they're amazing. (3) The stocking for my 150 gallon tank is here *at the weekend because of the clownloach i upgraded it to 200 an 200 gallon 8 inch clownloach 5 with an krib pairs fire mouth honey gourami 6 with 16 cory cats 5 australian rainbow of breeding angel fishes loach and 5 clown 1 inch*
Portuguese	(1) "Vivo num Estado de Ironia". (2) Gosto de levar a sério o meu papel de consultor encartado. (3) Na Holanda, Bélgica, Itália e Espanha, os números oscilam entre 250 mil e 300 mil muçulmanos.	(1) "vivia num estado de ironia". (2) Gosto de *levá* a sério a *seu* papel consultor de encartado. (3) *, nas e Espanha Holanda Itália, Bélgica,* os números oscilam entre 250 mil e 300 mil muçulmanos.
Spanish	(1) El IMIM sólo controla muestras remitidas por el COI y de competiciones extranjeras. (2) Tras la violación, la mujer fue a interponer una denuncia en comisaría, "pero como sufría hemorragias y pérdida de conocimiento, la propia policía llamó a una ambulancia y la envió al Hospital La Paz". (3) El COI abrió ayer, por orden de su presidente, el belga Jacques Rogge, una investigación al descubrir, por casualidad, material médico para realizar transfusiones, bolsas vacías de sangre y restos de glucosa en una casa alquilada, en Soldier Hollow, muy cerca de Salt Lake City, por el equipo de fondo de la Federación Austriaca de Esquí durante la disputa de los recientes JJOO.	(1) El IMIM sólo controla muestras remitidas por el COI y de competiciones extranjeras. (2) La mujer fue a interponer una denuncia en comisaría *tras la violación,"., pero,* como *sufriría* hemorragias y pérdida de conocimiento "la propia policía llamó a una ambulancia y la envió al Hospital La Paz (3) El COI abrió ayer *una investigación* por orden de su presidente, el belga Jacques Rogge,*, al descubrir, por casualidad, material médico, bolsas vacías de sangre y restos de glucosa para transfusiones realizamos* en una casa *alquilado* por el equipo de fondo de la Federación Austriaca de Esquí durante la disputa de los recientes JJOO, en Soldier Hollow, *mucho* cerca de Salt Lake City,.

Table 2: Examples of generation for English, Portuguese and Spanish

Ciências Matemáticas e de Computação - Universidade de São Paulo, Brasil.

George Doddington. 2002. Automatic evaluation of machine translation quality using n-gram co-occurrence statistics. In *Proceedings of the Second International Conference on Human Language Technology Research*, HLT '02, pages 138–145, San Francisco, CA, USA. Morgan Kaufmann Publishers Inc.

Nathan Hartmann, Erick Fonseca, Christopher Shulby,

Marcos Treviso, Jéssica Silva, and Sandra Aluísio. 2017. Portuguese word embeddings: Evaluating on word analogies and natural language tasks. In *Proceedings of the 11th Brazilian Symposium in Information and Human Language Technology*, pages 122–131. Sociedade Brasileira de Computação.

Eva Hasler, Felix Stahlberg, Marcus Tomalin, Adrià de Gispert, and Bill Byrne. 2017. A comparison of neural models for word ordering. In *Proceedings of the 10th International Conference on Natural Language Generation, INLG 2017, Santiago de Compostela, Spain, September 4-7, 2017*, pages 208–212.

Guillaume Klein, Yoon Kim, Yuntian Deng, Jean Senellart, and Alexander Rush. 2017. Opennmt: Open-source toolkit for neural machine translation. In *Proceedings of ACL 2017, System Demonstrations*, pages 67–72. Association for Computational Linguistics.

Philipp Koehn. 2005. Europarl: A Parallel Corpus for Statistical Machine Translation. In *Conference Proceedings: the tenth Machine Translation Summit*, pages 79–86, Phuket, Thailand. AAMT, AAMT.

Simon Mille, Anja Belz, Bernd Bohnet, Yvette Graham, Emily Pitler, and Leo Wanner. 2018. The First Multilingual Surface Realisation Shared Task (SR'18): Overview and Evaluation Results. In *Proceedings of the 1st Workshop on Multilingual Surface Realisation (MSR), 56th Annual Meeting of the Association for Computational Linguistics (ACL)*, pages 1–10, Melbourne, Australia.

Kishore Papineni, Salim Roukos, Todd Ward, and Wei-Jing Zhu. 2002. Bleu: A method for automatic evaluation of machine translation. In *Proceedings of the 40th Annual Meeting on Association for Computational Linguistics*, pages 311–318, Stroudsburg, PA, USA. Association for Computational Linguistics.

Jeffrey Pennington, Richard Socher, and Christopher Manning. 2014. Glove: Global Vectors for Word Representation. In *Proceedings of the 2014 Conference on Empirical Methods in Natural Language Processing (EMNLP)*, pages 1532–1543, Doha, Qatar. Association for Computational Linguistics.

Ehud Reiter and Robert Dale. 2000. *Building Natural Language Generation Systems*. Cambridge University Press, New York, NY, USA.

Allen Schmaltz, Alexander M. Rush, and Stuart M. Shieber. 2016. Word ordering without syntax. In *Proceedings of the 2016 Conference on Empirical Methods in Natural Language Processing*, pages 2319–2324. The Association for Computational Linguistics.

Milan Straka and Jana Straková. 2017. Tokenizing, pos tagging, lemmatizing and parsing ud 2.0 with udpipe. In *Proceedings of the CoNLL 2017 Shared Task: Multilingual Parsing from Raw Text to Universal Dependencies*, pages 88–99, Vancouver, Canada. Association for Computational Linguistics.

Ilya Sutskever, Oriol Vinyals, and Quoc V. Le. 2014. Sequence to sequence learning with neural networks. In *Proceedings of the 27th International Conference on Neural Information Processing Systems - Volume 2*, NIPS'14, pages 3104–3112, Cambridge, MA, USA. MIT Press.

Ramakrishna Vedantam, C. Lawrence Zitnick, and Devi Parikh. 2015. Cider: Consensus-based image description evaluation. In *IEEE Conference on Computer Vision and Pattern Recognition, CVPR 2015, Boston, MA, USA, June 7-12, 2015*, pages 4566–4575.

Yue Zhang and Stephen Clark. 2015. Discriminative syntax-based word ordering for text generation. *Computational Linguistics*, 41(3):503–538.

The DipInfo-UniTo System for SRST 2018

Valerio Basile
Dipartimento di Informatica
Università degli Studi di Torino
Corso Svizzera 185, 10153 Torino
valeriobasile@gmail.com

Alessandro Mazzei
Dipartimento di Informatica
Università degli Studi di Torino
Corso Svizzera 185, 10153 Torino
mazzei@di.unito.it

Abstract

This paper describes the system developed by the DipInfo-UniTo team to participate to the shallow track of the Surface Realization Shared Task 2018 (Mille et al., 2018). The system employs two separate neural networks with different architectures to predict the word ordering and the morphological inflection independently from each other. The UniTo realizer is language in dependent, and its simple architecture allowed it to be scored in the central part of the final ranking of the shared task.

1 Introduction

Natural Language Generation from formal structures, and in particular tree-like structures, has been approached with a variety of methods in the literature. For instance, SimpleNLG (Gatt and Reiter, 2009) takes as input a tree-like representation (a sort of *quasi*-syntactic tree enriched with a series of features) and produces an English sentence. SimpleNLG has is largely used in different NLG systems and has been ported to a number of different language (Italian among them (Mazzei et al., 2016)).

In the PhD thesis of Basile (2015), the generation process starts from a recursive representation of the semantics of a discourse (a Discourse Representation Structure, from Discourse Representation Theory) and it is carried out by transforming the original DRS into a directed graph (quite similar to a tree) aligned with the surface form at the word level. While the approach of Basile (2015) is aimed towards generation from abstract representations of meaning, in practice it is applicable to similar structures encoding information at a different level of abstraction, such as the trees that form the input of the present shared task.

We draw further inspiration from the aforementioned work in dividing the generation process into the word ordering prediction and morphology inflection generation. We follow a simplified approach by considering these two subtasks as independent from each other. We implement two modules based on neural networks that work in parallel, and whose output is later combined to produce the final surface form (cf. Figure 2).

In this paper we describe the the DipInfo-UniTo realizer (hencefort UniTO realizer) participating to the shallow track of the Surface Realization Shared Task 2018 (Mille et al., 2018).

In Section 2 we describe the system implemented from scratch for the word ordering subtask, and in Section 3 we briefly describe the deep learning-based approach that we used for the morphology inflection subtask. In Section 4 we describe the experimental pipelines used for training and testing the UniTo realizer and, moreover, we report the results on the test set. Finally, Section 5 closes the paper with some considerations and points to future developments.

2 Word Ordering

We adopted a *local ordering* approach to the task of predicting word ordering, as opposed to *global ordering*. We reformulate the problem of sentence-wise word ordering in terms of reordering its component subtrees, and subsequently recomposing the ordering of the words at the sentence level starting from the ordered subtrees.

The algorithm is composed of three steps: splitting the input unordered tree into single-level unordered subtrees (Section 2.1); predicting the local word order for each subtree (Section 2.2); recomposing the single-level ordered subtrees into a single multi-level ordered tree to obtain the global word order (Section 2.3).

Proceedings of the First Workshop on Multilingual Surface Realisation, pages 65–71
Melbourne, Australia, July 19, 2018. ©2018 Association for Computational Linguistics

2.1 Extracting Lists of Items to Rank from the Input Trees

In the first step, we split the original unordered universal dependency multilevel tree into a number of single-level unordered trees, where each subtree is composed by a head (the root) and all its dependents (the children), in a way similar to (Bohnet et al., 2012).

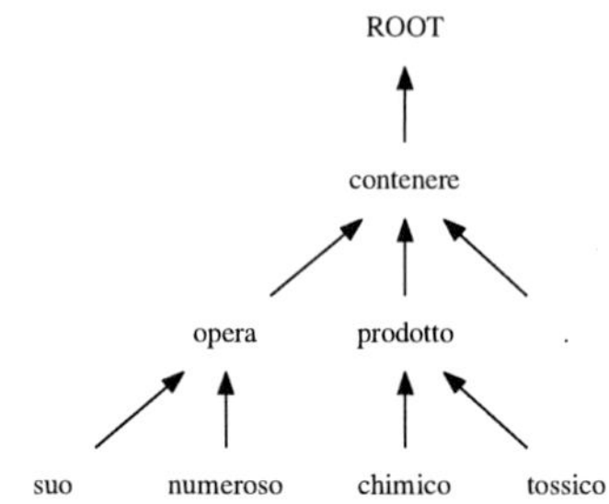

(a) Tree corresponding to the sentence in the Italian training set *"Numerose sue opere contengono prodotti chimici tossici."*

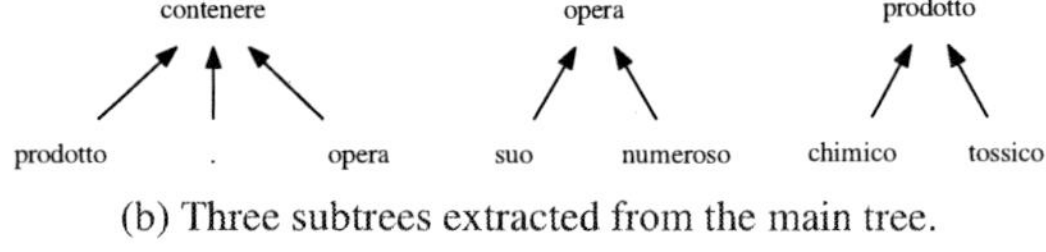

(b) Three subtrees extracted from the main tree.

contenere	opera	prodotto
prodotto	suo	chimico
.		opera
opera		tossico

(c) Three lists of items to order, corresponding to the three subtrees.

Figure 1: Illustration of the process of splitting the input tree into subtrees and extracting lists of items for learning to rank.

An example is shown in Figure 1: from the (un-ordered) tree representing the sentence *"Numerose sue opere contengono prodotti chimici tossici."* (1a), each of its component subtrees (limited to one-level dependency) is considered separarately (1b). The head and the dependents of each subtree form a list of unordered items (1c). Crucially, we leverage the flat structure of the subtrees in order to extract structures that are suitable as input to the learning to rank algorithm in the next step of the process.

As a consequence of the design of our approach, in some cases the correct word order cannot be predicted. In particular, this is the case for non-projective tree structures, because the only realizations allowed by the formalism are those deriv-ing from the dependency structure. For instance, the dependency tree representing the sentence *He gave a talk yesterday about generation* cannot be realized by the UniTo realizer since the tree itself is not projective. In this case, the best realization could be along the lines of *He gave yesterday a talk about generation.*

2.2 Supervised Learning to Rank

In the second step of the word ordering prediction algorithm, we predict the relative order of the head and the dependents of each subtree with a *learning to rank* approach. We employ the list-wise learning to rank algorithm *ListNet*, proposed in (Cao et al., 2007). The relatively small size of the lists of items to rank allows us to use a list-wise approach, as opposed to pairwise or point-wise approaches, while keeping the computation times manageable. Indeed, ListNet is a general-ized version of the pairwise learning to rank algo-rithm RankNet (Burges et al., 2005).

ListNet uses a list-wise loss function based on *top one probability*, i.e., the probability of an element of being the first one in the ranking. The top one probability model approximates the *permutation probability* model that assigns a probability to each possible permutation of an ordered list. This approximation is necessary to keep the problem tractable by avoiding the exponential explosion of the number of permutations.

Formally, the top one probability of an object j is defined as

$$P_s(j) = \sum_{\pi(1)=j, \pi \in \Omega_n} P_s(\pi)$$

that is, the sum of the probabilities of all the possible permutations of n objects (denoted as Ω_n) where j is the first element. $s = (s_1, ..., s_n)$ is a given list of *scores*, i.e., the position of elements in the list. Considering two permutations of the same list y and z (for instance, the predicted order and the reference order) their distance is computed using cross entropy. The distance measure and the top one probabilities of the list elements are used in the loss function:

$$L(y, z) = -\sum_{j=1}^{n} P_y(j) log(P_z(j))$$

The list-wise loss function is plugged into a lin-ear neural network model to provide a learning environment. ListNet takes as input a sequence of ordered lists of feature vectors (the features are encoded as numeric vectors). The weights of the network are iteratively adjusted by computing a list-wise cost function that measure the distance between the reference ranking and the prediction of the model and passing its value to the gradient descent algorithm for optimization of the parameters.

We used an implementation of ListNet[1] that was previously applied in a surface realization task with a similar supervised setting (Basile, 2015). On top of the core ListNet algorithm, this implementation features a regularization parameter to prevent overfitting.

The choice of features for the supervised learning to rank component is a critical point of our solution. We use several word-level features encoded as one-hot vectors:

- The universal POS-tag.

- The treebank specific POS tag.

- The morphology features and the head-status of the word (head of the single-level tree vs. leaf).

Furthermore, we included word representations, differentiating between content words and function words:

- For open-class word lemmas (content words) we added to the feature vector the corresponding specific language embedding from the pre-trained multilingual model Polyglot (Al-Rfou' et al., 2013).

- Closed-class word lemmas (function words) are encoded as one-hot bags of words vectors.

An implementation of the feature encoding for the word ordering module of our architecture is available online[2].

2.3 From Local Order to Global Order

We reconstruct the global (i.e. sentence-level) order from the local order of the one-level trees under the hypothesis of projectivity. If the local reordering of the one-level tree T_1^h with root h and children $c_1...c_M$ produces an order of nodes $n_1 n_2...n_{M+1}$, the hypothesis of projectivity implies that in the global word order the position of

all the children of the node n_j will be after the position of the node n_{j-1} and before the position of the node n_{j+1}. So, the node global order (O) of a k-level tree T_k^h rooted by the node h and with children $c_1...c_M$ can be rewritten formally in terms of the local order as:

$$O(T_k^h) = \begin{cases} h & \text{if } k=0 \\ O_{ln}(h, c_1, ..., c_M) & \text{if } k=1 \\ O_{ln}(h, O(T_{k-1}^{c_1}), ..., O(T_{k-1}^{c_M})) & \text{if } k>1 \end{cases}$$

where $O_{ln}(h, c_1, ..., c_M)$ is the permutation learned by the ListNet algorithm from the training set and parametrized over the feature set $F(h, c_1, ..., c_M)$ (cf. Section 2.2), that is

$$O_{ln}(h, c_1, ..., c_M) \stackrel{def}{=} P_{ListNet}^{F(h,c_1,...,c_M)}(h, c_1, ..., c_M)$$

3 Morphology Inflection

For the task of morphological inflection prediction, we implemented a module to work in parallel with the word order module described previously. This component of the system considers the morphology inflection as an alignment problem between characters that can be modeled with the sequence to sequence paradigm.

We used a deep neural network architecture based on a hard attention mechanism. The model has been recently introduced by Aharoni and Goldberg (2017) and showed state-of-the-art performance on several morphological inflection benchmarks. The model consists of a neural network in an encoder-decoder setting. However, at each step of the training, the model can either write a symbol to the output sequence, or move the attention pointer to the next state of the sequence. This mechanism is meant to model the natural monotonic alignment between the input and output sequences, while allowing the freedom to condition the output on the entire input sequence.

We trained the system[3] on the SRST training data set with no particular parameter tuning, that is, adopting an "off-the-shelf" approach. Moreover, we used a straight approach by using all the morphological features provided by the original UD treebank annotation and the dependency relation binding the word to its head. So, in the training pipeline (Figure 2), we

[1]https://github.com/valeriobasile/listnet

[2]https://github.com/alexmazzei/ud2ln

[3]An implementation of the model by Aharoni and Goldberg (2017) is freely available as https://github.com/roeeaharoni/morphological-reinflection

transform the training files into a set of structures $((lemma, features), form)$ in order to learn the neural inflectional model associating a $(lemma, features)$ to the corresponding $form$. The neural inflectional model is exploited in the test pipeline in order to compute the $form$ corresponding to a specific $(lemma, features)$ in the test file.

4 Experiments

Since our approach does not rely on language specific procedures or hand-made rules, we have initially planned to train the UniTo realizer for all the ten languages proposed by the SRST organizers. However, because of time constraints, we decided to focus on four specific languages first: English, Spanish, French and Italian (EN-ES-FR-IT). In particular, for English, French and Italian the learning time for word ordering and morphology inflection was around 36 and 24 hours respectively[4]. In contrast, for Spanish language, which has a considerable larger learning file, the learning time was approximatively doubled.

4.1 Pipelines

We designed two processing pipelines for the training phase and testing phase as depicted in Figure 2. We applied separately four times both the pipelines for the four tested languages EN-ES-FR-IT.

In the training pipeline, we created two distinct files starting from the UD treebank training files. The first file contains morphological information (that is $((lemma, features), form)$, cf. Section 3) and it is used to create the morphological inflection model by using the deep learning architecture described in Section 3. The second file contains the vector representation of the tree features (embeddings or function words, morphological features, etc., cf. Section 2.2) and it is used to create the word order model by using the linear neural network architecture described in Section 2.

In the testing pipeline, we created two distinct files starting from the test files provided from the organizers. Both files are created with the same procedures of the training pipelines. The first file was used to test the morphological neural model and to create a mapping from the pair lemma-features to the inflected form. The second file

---

was used to test the word order neural model by providing the local word orders for the subtrees and the word order at the sentence level (cf. Section 2.3). In a subsequent step, the information from the morhological map and from the word ordered trees are merged into one single complete and CONLL compliant tree structure. Finally, the trees are detokenized (see 4.3) in order to produce the sentences that are submitted as the final output of the system.

4.2 Datasets

The rules of the shallow track for the SRST 2018 allowed to use any resource to train the surface realizers. However, in order to investigate about the syntactic information contained in the Universal Dependency format and its appropriateness for NLG tasks, we decided to use mostly information derived from the project Universal Dependency (Nivre et al., 2016). Indeed, the only exception regards the encoding of the open classes words in terms of language specific pre-compiled embeddings for the word order model (Al-Rfou' et al., 2013) (cf. Section 2.2)).

The task organizers provided ten training and ten development files derived from the version 2.1 of the UD dataset for the ten languages included in the shallow track. Indeed, they provided a modified versions of the original treebanks in which the information about the inflected word form was removed and, the original word order was replaced with a random order. Additionally, the organizers provided ten text files containing the sentences of the treebank in their original form.

However, we noted that the training files provided by the organizers had an unresolvable ambiguity in the case of a sentence containing the same lemma multiple times. As a consequence, we decided to use the original versions 2.1 of the treebank files since they contain both the gold word order and the inflected forms of the word. During the conversion of the dependency trees into a vector form (see Section 2), we ignored the information about word ordering and inflected forms.

For English, Spanish and French, we used the training files developed in the English, Spanish-AnCora, and French main UD treebanks respectively. In contrast, for Italian we built a new training file by merging together the training file of the Italian main UD treebank with the training files of the UD Italian treebanks Italian-PUD, Italian-

68

---

⁴The experiments were run on two distinct multi-core PCs with GNU/Linux operating systems and GPU computing capabilities

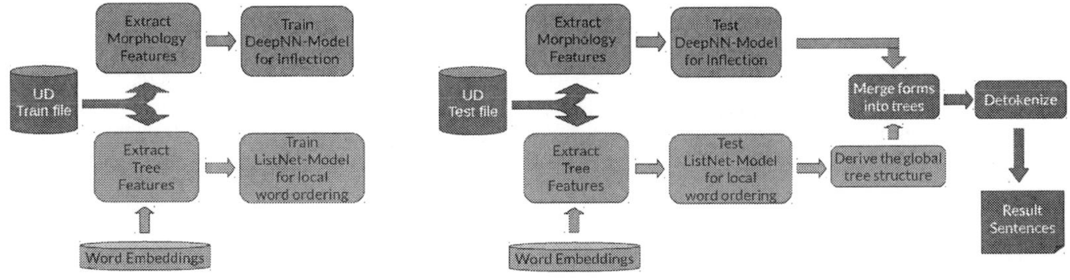

Figure 2: The training and testing pipelines.

ParTUT and Italian-PoSTWITA.

4.3 Detokenization

In order to produce the final result of the realization one needs to transform the UD tree produced by the UniTo realizer into a single string containing the sentence. Since the final goal of the task was to reproduce an output sentence close to the original sentence used by the treebanks developers, we needed to post-process the tree with additional two phases, that are *contraction* and *space removal*.

Contraction In this phase the sentence was modified in order to produce the contracted form for some specific multi-word constructions. In particular, for Spanish, French and Italian, there are two linguistic phenomena to account for, that are *articulated preposition* and *clitics*.

For instance, Italian provides a morphological mechanism to contract prepositions and articles into articulated prepositions. Indeed, there are 7 Italian simple prepositions (*di* (of), *a* (to), *da* (from), *in* (in), *con* (with), *su* (on)) which contract with the article. For instance, *la casa della zia* (the house of-the aunt) = la + casa + della (di [preposition] + la [definite article feminine singular]) + zia. In a similar way, clitics are pronouns which in Italian in particular cases can be included in the verb form, like in *Dammi la mela* (Give-me the apple) = Dammi (dai [verb] + me [pronoun]) + la + mela.

Since they are special case of multiwords, both articulated prepositions and clitics have a special annotation status into UD treebanks. Indeed, there is a line containing the multiword indexed with integer ranges, like *della* 3-4, and additional lines with single tokens annotation, like *di* 3 and *la* 4. We exploit this annotation by automatically extracting from the EN-ES-FR-IT UD treebanks all the regular expressions that are necessary to recompose the multiwords from the tokens (e.g. the PERL regular expression *s/ di la / della /gi*). By using the UD treebanks training files of EN-ES-FR-IT we found 0^5, 923, 9, and 920 regular expressions respectively.

Space Removal Each language has additional specific rules for the treatment of space between words and punctuations. In order to treat this specific cases we used the detokenizer script provided in the moses project[6]: the detokenizer provides specific rules for English, French and Italian[7].

4.4 Results

In Table 1 we report the quantitative evaluation provided by shared task organizers of the surface realizer. With respect to the other teams, our results score in the middle-lower part of the final ranking: 6th out of 8 according to the BLEU and NE DIST score, and 5th out of 8 according to NIST.

---

[5]English language does not have neither articulated preposition and clitics.

[6]`https://github.com/moses-smt/mosesdecoder/blob/master/scripts/tokenizer/detokenizer.perl`

[7]As approximation, we used Italian configuration for Spanish too.

	EN	ES	FR	IT	Av.
BLUE	23.20	26.90	23.12	24.61	9.78
NE DIST	51.87	24.53	18.04	36.11	13.06
NIST	8.86	9.58	7.72	8.25	3.44

Table 1: The performance in terms of BLUE, DIST and NIST scores of the UniTo Realizer. The average is computed by considering the mean over the ten languages proposed for the shallow track.

The BLUE scores obtained suggest that the UniTo realizer have the same performances for all four languages. In contrast, the NE DIST results shows a better performance on the English language with respect to the other languages. Since BLEU and NIST give stronger weight to word order and lexical choice respectively (Zhang et al., 2004), these results suggest that our word order and morphology inflection modules equally contribute to the result. The difference in the NE DIST performance across languages has been observed in the other participants' results, and it could be due to the different morphological profile of the English with respect to the romance languages (ES-FR-IT).

5 Conclusion and Future Work

In this paper, we described the main features of the UniTo realizer, the system adopted by the DipInfo-UniTo team to participate to the shallow track of the Surface Realization Shared Task 2018. We described the two main components of the realizer: a linear neural network used to solve the word ordering subtask, and a deep neural network used to solve the morphological inflection subtask.

A number of possible improvements could be applied to the architecture. For instance, the morphological inflection could consider features deriving from sequences of words, i.e., having the word ordering module to inform the morphology module, or the other way around. Moreover, additional experiments are necessary in order to obtain the best tuning of the hyperparameters involved in the training phase.

References

Roee Aharoni and Yoav Goldberg. 2017. Morphological inflection generation with hard monotonic attention. In *Proceedings of the 55th Annual Meeting of the Association for Computational Linguistics, ACL 2017*, pages 2004–2015.

Rami Al-Rfou', Bryan Perozzi, and Steven Skiena. 2013. Polyglot: Distributed word representations for multilingual nlp. In *CoNLL*, pages 183–192. ACL.

Valerio Basile. 2015. *From Logic to Language : Natural Language Generation from Logical Forms*. Ph.D. thesis, University of Groningen, Netherlands.

Bernd Bohnet, Anders Björkelund, Jonas Kuhn, Wolfgang Seeker, and Sina Zarrieß. 2012. Generating non-projective word order in statistical linearization. In *Proceedings of the 2012 Joint Conference on Empirical Methods in Natural Language Processing and Computational Natural Language Learning*, pages 928–939. Association for Computational Linguistics.

Chris Burges, Tal Shaked, Erin Renshaw, Ari Lazier, Matt Deeds, Nicole Hamilton, and Greg Hullender. 2005. Learning to rank using gradient descent. In *Proceedings of the 22Nd International Conference on Machine Learning*, ICML '05, pages 89–96, New York, NY, USA. ACM.

Zhe Cao, Tao Qin, Tie-Yan Liu, Ming-Feng Tsai, and Hang Li. 2007. Learning to rank: From pairwise approach to listwise approach. In *Proceedings of the 24th International Conference on Machine Learning*, ICML '07, pages 129–136, New York, NY, USA. ACM.

Albert Gatt and Ehud Reiter. 2009. Simplenlg: A realisation engine for practical applications. In *Proceedings of the 12th European Workshop on Natural Language Generation*, ENLG '09, pages 90–93, Stroudsburg, PA, USA. Association for Computational Linguistics.

Alessandro Mazzei, Cristina Battaglino, and Cristina Bosco. 2016. Simplenlg-it: adapting simplenlg to italian. In *INLG 2016 - Proceedings of the Ninth International Natural Language Generation Conference, September 5-8, 2016, Edinburgh, UK*, pages 184–192.

Simon Mille, Anja Belz, Bernd Bohnet, Yvette Graham, Emily Pitler, and Leo Wanner. 2018. The First Multilingual Surface Realisation Shared Task (SR'18): Overview and Evaluation Results. In *Proceedings of the 1st Workshop on Multilingual Surface Realisation (MSR), 56th Annual Meeting of the Association for Computational Linguistics (ACL)*, pages 1–10, Melbourne, Australia.

Joakim Nivre, Marie-Catherine de Marneffe, Filip Ginter, Yoav Goldberg, Jan Hajic, Christopher D. Manning, Ryan T. McDonald, Slav Petrov, Sampo Pyysalo, Natalia Silveira, Reut Tsarfaty, and Daniel Zeman. 2016. Universal dependencies v1: A multilingual treebank collection. In *Proceedings of the Tenth International Conference on Language Resources and Evaluation LREC 2016, Portorož, Slovenia, May 23-28, 2016*.

Ying Zhang, Stephan Vogel, and Alex Waibel. 2004. Interpreting bleu/nist scores: How much improvement do we need to have a better system. In *In Proceedings of Proceedings of Language Resources and Evaluation (LREC-2004*, pages 2051–2054.

Author Index